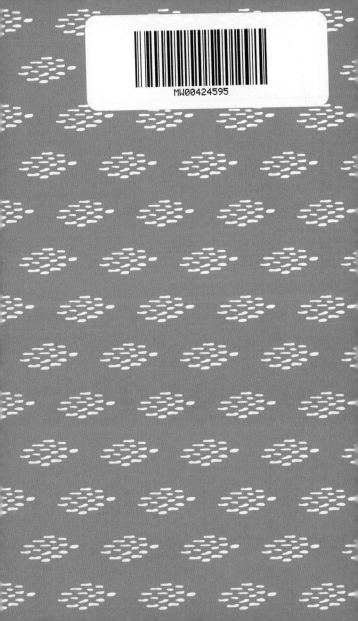

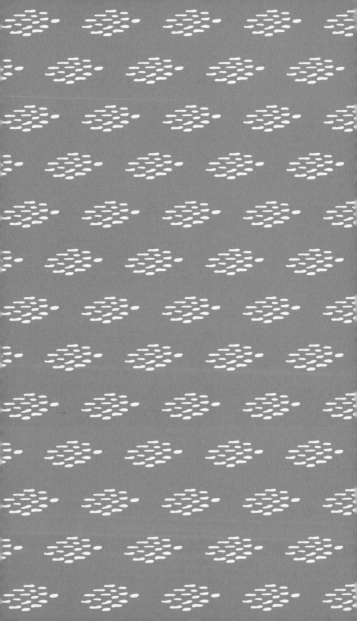

To

_____

From

_____

Date

_____

Goodbye, tension! Hello, pension!

You make known to me the path of life; in your presence there is fullness of joy; at your right hand are pleasures forevermore.

PSALM 16:11 ESV

When you think of the word retirement, what comes to mind? Lazy days lounging around the house in your PJs? A fishing pole and a rowboat? Hitting the road in an RV? This new season of your life might be the opportunity to do all these things and many more.

Retirement is the ultimate re- word. Re- is a prefix that indicates a do-over. Isn't that just what your retirement years should be—a chance to reimagine your life, to reinvent yourself, and to rediscover who you were called to be? So, let's break this down.

Re-: again
Tire: to grow weary and look forward to rest

Your retirement season is meant to be an opportunity to step away from the exhaustion, move out of the rat race, and settle into a season of refreshing. It's also a chance to give in to the temptation to slow down. (Hey, slowing down is a good thing, you know!)

So, how do you kick off this special season? With joy, excitement, and anticipation that the Lord will truly move! Let this fun devotional serve as a springboard for this season of adventure. And as you dive into the opportunities ahead, use the stories and devotions in this little book to convince yourself that you're not alone.

You're not, after all! God has walked with you from the beginning, and He's got great plans for you even now. In fact, with your thoughts finally freed up from the day-in, day-out workload, the Lord can have your undivided attention! Not that you won't fill up those hours with other things. There are terrific options for the retiree, after all. In the words of Mr. Rogers: *"Often when you think you're at the end of something, you're at the beginning of something else."*

RETIREMENT ROCKS!

Devotions for All That Free Time

DaySpring
LIVE YOUR FAITH

Contents

Rediscover..8

Sentimental Journey..10

As Time Goes By 12

Come Fly with Me 14

Ain't No Mountain High Enough 16

My Favorite Things...18

Release 22

It's Now or Never 24

Big Girls (and Boys) Don't Cry...............................26

Stop! In the Name of Love.......................................28

Wouldn't It Be Nice 30

It Only Hurts for a Little While 32

Reinvent...36

Come On-a My House..38

Wake Up Little Susie...40

A Change Is Gonna Come 42

Blue Suede Shoes...44

When I'm Sixty-Four 46

Relationships...50

I Got You Babe 52

You Make Me Feel So Young....................................54

Yakety Yak 56

I'll Be Seeing You 58

Puppy Love 60

Rethink..64

Contents

Don't Fence Me In 66

Ain't That a Kick in the Head? 68

It's Your Thing 70

Daydream Believer 72

For Once in My Life 74

Reality 78

You Can't Always Get What You Want 80

Sugar, Sugar 82

Twist and Shout 84

They Can't Take That Away from Me 86

I Fall to Pieces 88

Dazed and Confused 90

Reengage 94

Papa's Got a Brand New Bag 96

Hit the Road Jack 98

Send Me a Postcard 100

Like a Rolling Stone 102

Beyond the Sea 104

Relax 108

It Is Well with My Soul 110

The Sound of Silence 112

Sittin' on the Dock of the Bay 114

Tossin' and Turnin' 116

Seasons in the Sun 118

Redo 122

Contents

The Good, the Bad, and the Ugly 124

These Boots Are Made for Walkin' 126

Happy Together 128

If I Were a Rich Man 130

Memories Are Made of This 132

Rededicate 136

That Lucky Old Sun 138

My Generation 140

Stop and Smell the Roses 142

All You Need Is Love 144

Don't Take Away the Music 146

Revive 150

Till the End of Time 152

One Day at a Time 154

I Get a Kick Out of You 156

Trust in the Lord 158

Who Wrote the Book of Love? 160

Reawaken 164

Hey, Good Lookin' 166

Band of Gold 168

Whole Lotta Shakin' Goin' On 170

Return to Me 172

What a Wonderful World 174

Rediscover

There is a whole new kind of life ahead, full of experiences just waiting to happen. Some call it "retirement"; I call it bliss.
BETTY SULLIVAN

The retirement years provide the perfect opportunity to rediscover: who you are, where you're headed, the things you enjoy, and for some, opportunities for blossoming romance. It's also a season where the Lord can help you discover a greater depth in your relationship with Him.

Instead of mourning the shifts in your life, begin to look at this season as a time of great adventure! It is, you know! Let's break down the word rediscover to find the possibilities!

Re-: again
Discover: to find something unexpectedly

When you open yourself up to rediscovery, you're saying, "Lord, let's do it again. Open my eyes to the wonders around me. I want to be in discovery mode every single day, to tap back into that sense of adventure I once experienced all those years ago. I don't want to miss a thing—from a child's first steps to the beauty of a colorful sunset." (How fun to live like that!)

Okay, sure . . . you might live in the same house, have the same spouse you've lived with for forty-plus years, even eat the same types of food. But the potential to rediscover the joy in those things is fresh, new, and exciting! So, look ahead with great anticipation in your heart. God wants you in discovery mode during your retirement years!

Picture yourself as a small child looking at creation with wonderment in your expression. Every discovery will point you in the direction of your Creator, who longs for you to rediscover Him during this season of your life too! And isn't that the finest way to live after all—wide-eyed and giddy over His creation? That sort of adventure can be yours for the taking now that you've retired. You've got the time. Now, get busy living!

Lord, thank You for putting me in discovery mode once again. I don't want to waste this precious season of my life. It's such an amazing gift, after all! Amen.

Sentimental Journey

"For I know the plans I have for you," declares the LORD, "plans for welfare and not for evil, to give you a future and a hope."
JEREMIAH 29:11 ESV

I 've got it all mapped out." Joe pulled out the page he'd just printed and showed it to his wife, Teresa. "A five-year-plan, a ten-year-plan, and even a twenty-year-plan."

"How long do you think we're going to live, anyway?" Teresa asked and then chuckled. "And why are we planning out all our days? I haven't even decided what I'm going to make for dinner tonight and you've got a plan for twenty years from now?"

"I just think it's good to be prepared, honey."

"Well sure, but if everything is laid out on paper, what happens if God takes us in a different direction? What if we randomly decide to move to Hawaii or Alaska?"

"Don't be silly." With the wave of a hand Joe dismissed her foolish ideas. He knew exactly where they were going to live and had even figured out all their expenses in advance. Didn't she see this was best, to be prepared?

"Joe, I'm not saying you're obsessed." She paused to clear her throat. "I'm just saying that we need to trust God to handle our future. We don't have to map out every single detail. Where's your sense of adventure, honey? I want to have the freedom to shift gears if He nudges us to do so."

Maybe Teresa had a point! Planning ahead is great, but don't ever forget, God already sees well into the future and has it all under control. He wants you to be prepared for the years ahead, so having a strategy is great. But don't forget to let go of the reins just enough to allow Him to move you in a different direction, should the need arise. He wants you to rediscover the kind of relationship with Him that allows you to fully hope, fully trust, and fully anticipate great things ahead.

Are you ready, friend? Your plans look great! But God's? They look even better!

Lord, I get it! You want me to be prepared for this season of my life, but You also want me to remember who's really in charge. As I learn to trust You more, I'll release this tight-fisted grip on my plans and give You the freedom to lead me as You see fit. Amen.

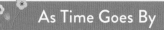

As Time Goes By

Teach us to number our days, that we may
gain a heart of wisdom.
PSALM 90:12 NIV

Carol rolled over in the bed and stretched. From the floor below, her black-and-tan dachshund let out a whimper.

"I know, boy," Carol said as she peered down at him. "You want to go out. I get it."

She, on the other hand, was thoroughly enjoying her lazy morning in bed. In fact, she'd gotten quite used to it since her retirement a few weeks back. No longer a slave to the alarm clock, she rather enjoyed sleeping in until the sun had fully risen. After years of stressful mornings, she was finally free to relax.

If only Copper would give her a break, she'd go on lounging even more. But the insistent pooch wouldn't wait any longer, so Carol finally forced herself from the bed. Her feet hit the cold floor and she hesitated. Then again, with the tiny pup's eyes gazing straight at her, she could hardly back out now. But once she walked outside, the cool breeze and the beautiful landscape, along with the smile and good-morning wave from her neighbor, well, it made getting out of those covers worth it.

Maybe you've been there. After years of early, rushed mornings, you're finally free to sleep in, to get that much-needed rest! You've earned it, for sure! Lazy mornings are wonderful, aren't they? Oh, the bliss of not being tied to an alarm clock!

Still, life is worth living. Sure, you're facing a lifetime of endless Saturdays, but Saturday was always your favorite day anyway. Right? So, bounce out of bed! There's life to be lived. Adventures to be had. God wants you to rediscover the joy of living, and that's hard to do when you're snuggled under the covers.

Lord, I have so much discovering to do! I'm so grateful for the additional time to rest and get refreshed, but I don't want to spend too much time snoozing the days away when You have so much out there for me to experience. Thank You for the joy of rediscovering how to spend my days! Amen.

Come Fly with Me

The LORD will keep your going out and your
coming in from this time forth and forevermore.
PSALM 121:8 ESV

Donna gazed at the digital map and tried to figure out a plan of action. If she and Louise made New Braunfels, Texas, the first stop on their road trip and then cut up through the country, they could stop at a wonderful little outlet mall she'd heard about. And from there they could take a scenic drive to Brenham, Texas. Maybe they could visit the ice cream factory when they got there. Yum. Or that Antique Rose Emporium. It sounded lovely.

Maybe you're like Donna. You're in discovery mode. Every road trip presents a unique opportunity to explore—new places, stores, restaurants, and all that nature has to offer. You're snapping photos of flowers and pausing to drink in the gorgeous views. You're lingering in antique shops and enjoying hole-in-the-wall restaurants recommended by locals in places you've never visited before. You're having intimate conversations with friends, going deeper than you ever have. And you're doing it all on your time, drinking in the wonder of the world around you.

In short, you're on a journey to rediscover God's creation—all the parts you didn't have time for before. And you're having a blast while doing it.

Isn't that just like God, to give you an adventure like this? He's so good! Your precious heavenly Father longs to energize you in new and fresh ways and give you a perspective like His—one that sees the world in all its splendor and glory. (It's pretty amazing, after all! Just look around you and you'll see how remarkable this planet really is!)

What parts of the world are you ready to rediscover? Where will you begin? Put on your adventure cap and start mapping out a plan! There are plenty of fun roads ahead.

Lord, thank You for showing me that I can rediscover the world around me! There are places I've not been, people I've not seen, things I've not done. It's not too late! I'm ready to step out into the great adventure that You have ahead for me.
Amen.

Ain't No Mountain High Enough

God's gifts and his call are irrevocable.
ROMANS 11:29 NIV

Bob leaned against the RV and flashed a grin in his daughter's direction. "Tell me your thoughts, Brenda. I can take it." He waited for her response but anticipated critique, not enthusiasm.

"I think it's a great idea, Pop," Brenda said, her eyes sparkling with excitement. "I mean, I'll miss you. The kids will miss you. But you and Mom will have a terrific time helping build churches. If this is what you feel the Lord is calling you to do, then how could I question it?"

"Thank you, honey. We will have a terrific time. I can tell you that we're already having a blast, just with the preparation." He grinned as joy flooded over him. "I haven't been this excited since I was a kid with my first bicycle."

"I'll bet."

"And the best news is, we'll be traveling with old friends and meeting new ones all at the same time. We're going to start at a little wood-framed church in Valdosta, Georgia, and move on from there to Biloxi, Mississippi. In all, our plan is to help build eight churches by mid-fall. We'll send you photos every step of the way. We'll probably even post them on social media."

"Wonderful!" Brenda gave her father an admiring look. "So, I guess you could say retirement is for the birds, then?"

"Sure is. There's still a lot of work left to be done, and I've got plenty of life left in me."

"And I'm sure it honors God to watch you minister to others, Pop. I'm so proud of you."

Doesn't Bob's story just thrill your soul? To think, the Lord was giving him an opportunity to rediscover his passion for service. He's got big plans for you too! Your finest days of service are ahead if you just open yourself up to the possibilities!

Thank You, heavenly Father, for opportunities and open doors! I can't wait to get started. Amen.

My Favorite Things

A person can do nothing better than to eat and drink
and find satisfaction in their own toil. This too, I see,
is from the hand of God, for without him, who can
eat or find enjoyment?
ECCLESIASTES 2:24–25 NIV

Mary glanced around her backyard and groaned. "Well, what do you think?" her husband asked as he rested against the handle of his shovel.

What did she think? Should she really tell him? Her once-pristine yard was now filled with blank patches of soil where Sonny planned to grow gardens. Lots of gardens, apparently. In the thirty-eight years they'd been married, the man had never once planted anything. Now it was all he could talk about.

"I think it's . . ." *Be nice, Mary.* "It's a blank canvas for your project. I'm sure you're going to have a lot of fun out here, honey." She offered what she hoped would look like an encouraging smile, but on the inside she wondered if, perhaps, he'd lost his marbles.

"We're going to have fun." Sonny flashed a wide grin and grabbed his shovel. "I can't wait for that new box garden to get here. Want to help me put it together? It'll be a great project."

"S-sure." She fought the temptation to shrug. Gardening was the last thing on her mind right now. Didn't Sonny see that she would rather be inside working on her quilting project?

Nope. Judging from the mischievous look in his eyes, he wanted her to play along. She would give it a try. Perhaps, in the end, she would grow to love gardening as much as quilting. And, she thought, it's never too late to try something new. Mary walked over, picked up a shovel, smiled at Sonny, and joined in the digging.

Maybe you can relate. You're in that fun season of life where everything seems new and fresh. Projects you've wanted to tackle for years (and projects you never thought you wanted to tackle) are now possible.

Be like Sonny and Mary. Dive right in. Give a new hobby a chance. Have fun digging that garden. There are plenty of hobbies to discover during this phase of your life after all. And look at it this way—if your latest great idea doesn't pan out, so what? You will have had an adventure trying something new. And there are plenty of other things to try should this gig not work out as you're hoping.

I'm ready for fun, new challenges, Lord! Set my mind free to imagine the possibilities! Amen.

Retirement Weekly Schedule:

Sunday—Whatever I Want to Do

Monday—Whatever I Want to Do

Tuesday—Whatever I Want to Do

Wednesday—Whatever I Want to Do

Thursday—Whatever I Want to Do

Friday—Whatever I Want to Do

Saturday—Whatever I Want to Do

RELEASE

Release

Brothers, I do not consider that I have made it my own. But one thing I do: forgetting what lies behind and straining forward to what lies ahead, I press on toward the goal for the prize of the upward call of God in Christ Jesus.
PHILIPPIANS 3:13–14 ESV

Letting go of the past isn't always easy, is it? No matter where you've come from—whether your yesterdays were blissful or tough—getting past them and moving on into a new phase of life can be complicated. God knows this, and He's planning to stick close so that you won't have to make the big decisions alone. In fact, He wants to be fully engaged every step of the way.

Before you fully move into your retirement years, perhaps it would be a good time to put the past behind you once and for all. This might involve releasing—people, memories, hopes, worries, fears . . . even relationships. No, it won't be easy. Yes, it will be worth it.

So, what does that look like? Break down the word release to find out!

Re-: again

Lease: to stay temporarily in a place you don't own, knowing it probably won't last forever

When you release your yesterdays to the Lord, you're saying, "It was never mine in the first place, Father. That job, that home, those possessions, those workplace friends . . . they were a temporary lease. And now You're offering me a new season, a new lease on life."

Most of all, a release means you've got to take your sticky fingers off it. This is never easy, but once you finally let go, peace will flood your soul, and you'll have a new perspective for the journey ahead.

Let it go, friend. It's hard to grab hold of today when you're still holding tightly to yesterday.

Letting go won't be easy, Lord, but I'm ready to release my yesterdays to You. Thanks for the reminder that they were never mine to begin with! Amen.

It's Now or Never

Do not boast about tomorrow, for you do not know what a day may bring.
PROVERBS 27:1 ESV

It's just so . . . weird." Carolyn stirred her tea and then leaned back against her café seat.

"What's weird?" her friend Jeanene asked.

"Being retired. Not knowing what tomorrow holds. I've always known what I was going to do on any given day, and now I don't." She shrugged and took a sip of her tea. Off in the distance a waitress served guests at a nearby table. She almost envied her. The work might be tiring, but at least that waitress knew what to expect from day to day.

"Are you bored or worried?" Jeanene asked.

Carolyn set the teacup down and paused to think through her friend's question. "Neither, really. I can't put my finger on it. I just like being in control of my days. When I had a job, I always knew what was coming next."

"Did you, though?" Jeanene gave her a pensive look. "Because none of us really knows what tomorrow holds. Maybe you're just missing the routine. Do you think that's it?"

That was it all right. Maybe what she needed was a new routine, one that would give her a sense of purpose again.

Can you relate to Carolyn's situation? Maybe you lived a very structured, routine life until you retired. You woke up at a certain time, drove to your job, had lunch at a certain time, drove home, had dinner, watched a show, and went to bed. Then the next day, you started all over again. Now you're confused. The day-in, day-out routine is no more. And though you enjoy the freedom, there's something to be said for knowing what's coming next.

Only, like Jeanene said, none of us really knows what's coming next in the grand scheme of things. So, set up your days if you like. Schedule them out with fun activities and hobbies. But remember, not knowing what's coming is truly part of the adventure, so you might as well relax and enjoy the ride!

I've been a creature of habit, Lord! I open myself up to new habits, new routines, and new adventures as I release the old ones to You! Amen.

Big Girls (and Boys) Don't Cry

I have been crucified with Christ and I no longer
live, but Christ lives in me. The life I now live in the
body, I live by faith in the Son of God, who loved
me and gave Himself for me.

GALATIANS 2:20 NIV

Karen looked through the photos on her phone, smiling as she came across the ones from her retirement party. How happy she'd looked that day. What joy and excitement she'd experienced.

Now, though? These pictures just caused a weird ache in her heart. In fact, she could hardly stand to look at them because they brought back so many memories. Did her friends at work even remember her anymore? Would they recognize the person she had become?

Truth be told, Karen struggled to know who she was outside of the workplace. After forty years in the insurance business, settling into a daily "I'm not working there anymore" routine hadn't come naturally. Most of her adult life she'd been known as Karen "Our Top Salesperson." Now she was just . . . Karen. And it stunk.

Maybe you know what it's like. You were at

the top of your game at your company. Everyone respected you. Revered you, even. It felt good to be admired. People aspired to be like you. Now you're just . . . you. And you don't know what that's supposed to look like or how it's supposed to feel.

Take a good look at today's verse. The life you live now—right now, in this very post-retirement moment—is lived by faith. That means you don't have to fully understand it all. You just have to recognize that your identity is—and always was—in Jesus, not yourself. What a relief, to know you don't have to work for it!

I'm so grateful my identity is in You, Lord! You're not asking me to jump through hoops or perform at a certain level. You love me just as I am! Amen.

Stop! In the Name of Love

Come to me, all who labor and are heavy laden,
and I will give you rest.
MATTHEW 11:28 ESV

"You don't have to do that, you know."

Katy looked up from scrubbing the baseboards and saw the concern in her husband's eyes as he stared down at her.

"Do what?" She swiped the perspiration from her forehead with the back of her hand.

"Clean all day. This house looks like it could be in a magazine already!" He took a bite of the apple in his hand and shrugged. "I'm just saying."

"Hardly!" She laughed and went back to work on the baseboards.

"Are you kidding? I saw my reflection in the refrigerator door just now. And the inside of the fridge smells like flowers. That's not natural. Throws a man off when his fridge smells like flowers."

"Maybe it's time to back away from the fridge, then, Stan." She reached for a different rag and concentrated on the spots on the baseboards. One of them wouldn't come off. Should she consider repainting the boards? Would that be a better option?

Worry lines creased Stan's forehead. "I'm just worried about you, Katy. You don't seem to know how to relax."

She stopped once again to think about his words as he headed off into the TV room. Maybe Stan had something there. She did seem driven these days. Ever since her retirement from the bank, she'd filled every hour of every day with some sort of activity—from housework to yardwork to cooking. And cooking. And cooking. The freezer was currently filled with enough prepared foods to last them for weeks to come. Okay, months, but who was counting?

Have you walked a mile in Katy's shoes? Are you finding it hard to relax since your retirement? Do you feel like you always need to be on the go?

Remember, even God took one day off! He's not keen on you working yourself to death! Let it go. Those baseboards? No one cares if they're speckled or clean. And for heaven's sake, don't paint them. There will be plenty of time for that later.

Teach me how to relax, Lord! I release my need to go, go, go! Amen.

Wouldn't It Be Nice

And my God will meet all your needs according to
the riches of His glory in Christ Jesus.
PHILIPPIANS 4:19 NIV

"You okay over there?"

Angela looked up from her cell phone into her daughter's eyes. "Oh, yes. Just checking on something." Truth be told, she couldn't stop worrying about her finances these days and kept checking her bank account. The balance was dropping, even as she spoke. If only she could slow the bleed, get things under control. Then she would stop fretting.

"Mom, are you going to be okay?" Megan asked. "I'm worried that you're worried."

Angela chose her words carefully, so as not to alarm her daughter. "Yes, I just have to get used to living on a budget. Now that I'm not working anymore, I don't have that paycheck deposit I came to count on."

"But you have your retirement, right?"

"Yes, it comes through on the first of the month."

"And Social Security?"

"It will start when I'm sixty-six years and seven months."

"Until then, are you going to be okay?" Now Megan looked genuinely concerned. "Because if you need help, you know that Matt and I will—"

Angela put her hand up. "I'll be fine. I don't know why I'm fretting. I really don't. I'm just having to trim back a little to make this work, is all. I'm not used to trimming back. I guess I was a little spoiled when I had a job."

"Well, don't worry about it today, okay?" Her daughter gestured to the restaurant table filled with food and the baby in the highchair nearby. "Today is all about us. And remember, lunch is on me, so don't worry about that."

"You don't need to do that."

"I know, but that makes it even more fun. So, relax, Mom."

Can you identify with Angela? Do your financial woes have you down? Release them to God and watch as He brings peace and teaches you a new way to live. Sure, this is a new season, but it's one where your heavenly Father will free you up to live by faith.

I give my finances to You, Lord! I'm done fretting.
Amen.

It Only Hurts for a Little While

Do not love the world or the things in the world. If anyone loves the world, the love of the Father is not in him. For all that is in the world—the desires of the flesh and the desires of the eyes and pride of life— is not from the Father but is from the world. And the world is passing away along with its desires, but whoever does the will of God abides forever.

I JOHN 2:15-17 ESV

Mike stared at the contents of his garage and groaned. When—and why—had he collected so much stuff? Sure, most of it was his wife's, but some of these things—like that old lawnmower in the corner, the one that needed a new carburetor—were nothing but junk. And if they were going to move to this new condo, he needed to figure out what to do with it and the other ten thousand pointless items he'd been collecting over the years.

Maybe you can relate to Mike's problem. Over the years you've taken in more and more stuff, jamming a lot of it into the garage. Or a storage shed. Or the closets. Now you're faced with a mountain of items, some of which were never unboxed, and others that were only used once or twice and then set aside.

There's no season like the retirement season to tackle all that, friend, especially if you're downsizing to a smaller space. You've got to look at it realistically, without emotion attached, and ask the question: "When will I use this . . . really?" If you're not sure of the answer, it's probably time to let it go.

Sure, it will hurt for a bit, but think about it this way: Jesus left the splendor of heaven to come to earth. There's not one verse listed in the Bible where you find Him complaining about all He left behind. He accepted His new venture and took it on willingly.

He's keen that you do the same. So, instead of being upset about all the stuff you need to find a place for, look at this season as the adventure it truly is! Releasing the old means embracing the new. And if you're moving forward with that same sense of curiosity and adventure in your heart, God will surprise you at every turn with the new!

Oh, and while you're at it, you might as well ditch that old lawnmower too. You know in your heart of hearts you're never going to use it at the new place.

I have too much stuff, Lord! Show me how and when to let it go. Amen.

HOW TO:

Live to a ripe old age:

Eat all the preservatives
you can.

REINVENT

Reinvent

I see retirement as just another of these
reinventions, another chance to do new things
and be a new version of myself.
WALT MOSSBERG

You're feeling the need to reinvent yourself, aren't you? Welcome to retirement! This is part of the process. You're certainly not alone in the desire to begin again. Maybe you've been identified as someone's mom or someone's dad for ages. Maybe you've always been "Meg's husband" or "Paul's wife." Perhaps you were "Top Salesman" at your job or kept the finest house in town. Today, though? You're ready for a change. Start by breaking down the word reinvent.

Re-: again
Invent: to produce something by using your
imagination or skills

You did it in the past. You were always creating something—a lovely home for your family, fun vacation adventures for the kids, financial goals. You were a busy bee! Now the situation is changing. Things are slowing down (at least in theory). But you're feeling an itch to reinvent yourself. You're in creative mode once again!

So, where will you begin? With your home? Your body? Your finances? Should you tackle your relationships? Your hobbies? Does one area get you more excited than others? Will you renovate your home, perhaps? Take up golf? Begin to look for newer, different activities? The possibilities are endless!

One word of advice: Don't look at this season as more work. You've had plenty of that! But there are certainly new ways to do things, and discovering them can be a blast. So, think of yourself like a chemist in a laboratory, cooking up something new. Invent new patterns, new plans, new spaces, and even new relationships, as the path opens wide before you.

Lord, I've always had an inquisitive mind! I've loved creating things over the years. Now it's time to reinvent myself, my space, and my attitude. I'll need Your help, but this is going to be a blast! No doubt about it. Amen.

Come On-a My House

By knowledge the rooms are filled with all
precious and pleasant riches.
PROVERBS 24:4 ESV

W ait, you're turning my old bedroom into . . .
a what?"

Kathleen laughed as she shifted the cell phone
to her other ear to respond to her daughter's
question. "A scrapbooking room, honey."

"I didn't know you were into scrapbooking,
Mom."

"I wasn't." Kathleen paused to looked at the
messy room. "Only, now I am. You should see all
the stuff I ordered online. I'm so excited." This led
to a lengthy chat about all her recent purchases—
everything from paper to stamping kits to ink. She
could hardly wait to get started!

"What does Dad think?" Courtney asked.

"Oh, he's so busy planting vegetables in the
garden behind the garage that he doesn't even
realize what I'm doing up here."

"Wait, we have a vegetable garden behind the
garage?"

"We do now!"

Maybe this story gave you a chuckle because you can relate. Parts of your home are changing—shifting from what they used to be to what they are now. Maybe you're accommodating incoming hobbies, or perhaps you're turning that old office into a guest room. Regardless, retirement is the perfect time to transform spaces, to repurpose them. That extra attic space? Maybe you can reinvent it, do something fun and different with it. That patch of ground behind the garage? Terrific box garden space. That spare bedroom? The decor from the eighties has to go. Maybe you could turn it into a quilting room.

Yep, there are plenty of things to keep you busy these days. So, look at everything with an inquisitive eye . . . and then dive right in.

I'm excited about the possibilities, Lord. I love to transform spaces. Give me excitement as I look at the many ways my home can become more usable to me during this season. Amen.

Wake Up Little Susie

If any of you lacks wisdom, you should ask God,
who gives generously to all without finding fault,
and it will be given to you.
JAMES 1:5 NIV

I've always been a night owl," Franky explained as he set his cup of coffee on the restaurant table. "Had to be. I worked the night shift. But these days?"

"You're confused?" his friend Ward asked.

"That's putting it mildly! My body doesn't know if I should be awake or asleep at any given time. So, I spend a lot of time going back and forth between the two. I need to get back on a regular schedule because I'm not getting enough rest, that's for sure." A yawn escaped, as if to prove his point. "If God does have a wife out there for me, she's going to have to put up with my crazy hours."

"Oh, I suspect she'll retrain you," Ward said and then laughed. "Spouses have a way of doing that, you know."

"I guess we'll see about that, if and when it ever happens." Franky picked up his cup of coffee, deep in thought.

Maybe you can relate. You've always been a morning person. Now you're off schedule. And you're doing that catch-as-catch-can approach to sleeping and waking—a couple of hours here, a couple of hours there. That's fine for a while, but you would feel better with consistent, steady rest.

So, what's a body to do? Set a new schedule and try to stick with it! Work with your natural body clock to determine the best time to sleep and wake. Don't worry! You'll settle into a routine if you give this part of your life to the Lord.

Lord, I know You care about my body clock. Help me do the necessary work to be in tip-top shape, well rested, and refreshed! Amen.

A Change Is Gonna Come

*Brothers and sisters, I do not consider myself
yet to have taken hold of it. But one thing I do:
Forgetting what is behind and straining toward
what is ahead, I press on toward the goal
to win the prize for which God has called me
heavenward in Christ Jesus.*
PHILIPPIANS 3:13-14 NIV

I remember when I weighed forty pounds less than I do right now." Fred sighed as he stared down at the bathroom scale. "How did it come to this?"

He knew the answer, of course. Those late-night bowls of ice cream. Popcorn loaded with butter and salt. That cheeseburger he'd just eaten for dinner. The french fries and sugary ketchup. The weight hadn't come on all at once, of course, but over the years he'd certainly added to his college weight.

"You can do it, Fred." His wife, Gloria, patted him on the back. "Just set a few goals for yourself and stick with a plan until you get there."

"Oh, it's as easy as all that, is it?" He stepped off the scale and shrugged. "Don't know why I didn't think of it myself!"

Maybe you can understand Fred's woes. You're hoping to drop a few pounds now that you've got extra time on your hands. But the idea of setting goals is hard. Sounds like too much work. And sticking with it? Even harder!

Whether you're hoping to lose weight, get your finances in order, or lay out a plan for a home renovation, setting goals is the answer. And it's a biblical answer! God has always been in the endgame business, after all. Consider today's verses from Philippians. We're not supposed to look backward. He wants us to press forward.

Pressing isn't always easy, especially when you're trying to change your health, your finances, or your relationships, but it's always worth it. So, set those goals. Then do as Gloria suggested: Make a plan and stick with it. Yep, it's really that simple!

Lord, thank You for the reminder that I need to set some goals. Show me the areas of my life that need the most work, then give me gentle nudges in the right direction so that changes can come! Amen.

Blue Suede Shoes

Do you not know that your bodies are temples
of the Holy Spirit, who is in you, whom you have
received from God? You are not your own;
you were bought at a price. Therefore
honor God with your bodies.
I CORINTHIANS 6:19-20 NIV

"This old body of mine ain't what it used to be."
Danielle shifted her position on the floor as she
tried to keep up with the woman on the video.

"C'mon, Danielle! You can do it." Her best
friend, Linda, spoke up from the spot next to her
on the living room floor. "We agreed we'd do this
exercise program together, remember?"

"That was before I realized they wanted me to
get down on the floor. Once I get down, girl . . . well,
you know."

"Yeah, I know. It's hard to get back up again."
Linda laughed and then adjusted her position.
"Ouch. That hurt."

"Tell me about it." Danielle sighed. "Next time
let's just go out for donuts and skip the workout.
Okay?"

Maybe you're like Danielle. It's been a while

since you've worked out. And now that you're retired, you know you should spend more time staying active. Your intentions are good. But your follow-through? Not so much!

Here's a fun thought: God has a lot for you to do. The journey ahead is going to be great fun. And it can be even better if you have a friend who is going through the hard changes with you. No, you're not in your twenties anymore. There are parts of you that creak and groan. But if you have someone on the floor next to you, it makes life more fun. Call a friend today and invite them to join you in a weekly activity—walking the dog, swimming at the community center, or joining an exercise class. Most of all, don't forget to laugh with each other on the donut days.

Lord, point me in the right direction. Who should I invite to join me? What activity should we do? As always, I want to follow Your plan for my life, even when it comes to fun weekly appointments. Amen.

When I'm Sixty-Four

For where your treasure is,
there your heart will be also.
MATTHEW 6:21 ESV

It's not too late to whip this into shape, you know."
George looked up from the spreadsheet and
fought the temptation to groan as his older brother
spoke.

"I wish I'd done a better job years ago. Started
putting more money aside. Invested wisely. I'm
feeling like a real slouch right now for not being
more on top of things."

Mark offered him a sympathetic look. "You can
only go forward from here. And hey, I'm a few miles
ahead of you on this journey, so I'm here to offer
sage advice, if you want to take it."

"Sure," George responded, grateful for the
offer. "I need all the help I can get. I've been feeling
pretty . . ."

"Overwhelmed? Hopeless? Scared?"

"All the above," George acknowledged. It
felt good to get this off his chest, actually. Having
someone else in the loop meant he was no longer
alone in this problem.

"Been there, done that. There were plenty of leaks in my proverbial boat, but I've plugged 'em all now, and I'm happy to help you do the same."

Maybe you're like George. You wish you'd paid more attention to finances when you were young. Wish you'd shopped less and invested more. Now it's time to pay the piper. You've retired, but you're worried about how you and your spouse will survive. She's got aspirations of traveling. She's already mapped out your first big trip, in fact. But you're worried about paying the electric bill.

Mark is right. You can only go forward from here. There's no point in beating yourself up over the mistakes you made in the past. You can always get things back on track.

It's hard to acknowledge what I won't even look at, Lord. Help me to tackle the hard things with eyes wide open! Amen.

HOW TO:

Exercise like a lazy person:

Do diddly-squats.

RELATIONSHIPS

Relationships

*Therefore encourage one another and build one
another up, just as you are doing.*
I THESSALONIANS 5:11 ESV

Your retirement years are the perfect time to
rebuild relationships. Whether you're hoping
to strengthen your marriage, further develop your
friendships, or build on those existing relationships
with your grown children, it's not too late. This should
be a season of encouraging others, of helping them
grow. God longs for you to truly relate to those in
your circle—not just in a passive way, but in a life-
changing one!

So, what does it mean to relate to someone?
Let's break it down.

Re-: again
Relate: to make or show a connection between;
to be connected or to have dealings with

Let's face it, some relationships just coast
along. Parents barely speak to their kids. Husbands
and wives exist in the same home but don't really
connect. Friends hang on the fringes, hardly seeing
or speaking to each other.

Your retirement years offer opportunities to break through those barriers and develop real, honest relationships. Building them isn't always easy. Sometimes making yourself vulnerable can help you connect to someone. Strangely, this can be toughest for those in a long-term marriage. (Hey, you know it's true! Some folks get so comfortable, so sloppy, that they stop trying to make genuine connections.) And it's not always easy for parents to know how to connect with their grown children. (Sometimes people grow apart, after all.) But you can't stop trying.

God wants more for you. He wants deeper, longer, stronger relationships for you. So, use this season to do the hard work and build, build, build those relationships. Again. And again. And again. And while you're at it, remember . . . God wants you to work on your relationship with Him too!

Lord, I can see that building relationships is going to require something of me. It might not be easy (and I'm not always keen on putting myself out there emotionally), but I'm willing to try. Help me build stronger relationships, I pray. Amen.

I Got You Babe

The LORD God said, "It is not good for the man to be alone. I will make a helper suitable for him."

GENESIS 2:18 NIV

I can't shake him," Twila whispered.

"Shake who?" Her best friend, Bonnie Sue, looked over from sorting through the cans of food with an inquisitive look on her face.

"John. My husband. I can't shake him."

Bonnie Sue put her hands on her hips. "Now, why would you want to do that?"

Twila looked around to make sure none of the other ladies working in the church's food pantry were close enough to hear. "You don't understand. Ever since he retired, he's everywhere. In my kitchen. In the living room. Leaving a mess in the bathroom. I go out to the garage . . . and he's there. I open the door to the bathroom . . . and he's there. I literally can't shake the man. He's everywhere."

Bonnie Sue laughed so hard that a couple of the other ladies headed their way. Well, great.

"I get it," Bonnie Sue said after Twila calmed down. "You're not used to him being home all day."

"Every. Single. Minute. Of. Every. Single. Day."

The other ladies laughed . . . and then swapped stories, one after the other.

"Buy him a golf membership," one friend suggested.

"Say yes every time he wants to buy a new tool," another added.

"Encourage him to build a man cave!" Bonnie Sue chimed in.

In that moment, Twila realized she was not alone in her struggle. For, while she loved and appreciated John, this current season was about to drive her bonkers.

Maybe you can relate. You're in a 24/7, 365-day-a-year relationship with your spouse. Or your elderly parent. Or an adult child who's living with you. And it's not easy. You wonder if you'll make it.

Deep breath! Take some time for yourself, by yourself, with yourself. Break away long enough to appreciate that person more when you come back. And remember, you're not "stuck with" that loved one. You're blessed to have them, whether you can see it now or not!

Lord, help me to change my perspective! I don't want to grow bitter simply because my situation at this moment is rough! Amen.

May you see your children's children!
Peace be upon Israel!
PSALM 128:6 ESV

"Slow down, kids! Grandma can't keep up!" Jenny huffed as she trudged down the sidewalk behind her three granddaughters. They were apparently very anxious to get to the neighborhood pool. She was anxious, too, but not in the same way. Appearing in public in a bathing suit was something she hadn't done for a while, and definitely not in front of the grandkids. Still, she would do anything for them.

Once they all got in the pool, everyone had a terrific time, Jenny included. In fact, she had such a good time that she didn't realize it was after five o'clock. Time to get home and start dinner. Strangely, the kids hadn't even noticed her chubby thighs or jiggly upper arms. If so, they certainly hadn't mentioned it.

"Race you home, Grandma?" seven-year-old Emma asked after they had dried off.

"I promise, that's not a race I'll win." Jenny gave her a wink. "But give me a few weeks and I'll give you a run for your money."

54

Maybe you've walked—er, run—a mile in Jenny's shoes. You've got little ones in your life and they're filling your post-retirement days with antics. You can hardly keep up! But you wouldn't trade this season for anything in the world. They're only young once, after all. And they need you. That much is clear.

That said, you're also learning how to set clear boundaries so that you can truly enjoy them when you're together. (Hey, too much of a good thing can still be too much, right?) So, give 'em all the hugs and kisses you like, feed 'em the yummy stuff, then send 'em back to Mom and Dad to raise.

Thanks for putting kids in my life, Lord! They definitely keep me young! (And tired!) Amen.

Yakety Yak

Two are better than one, because they have a good
return for their labor: If either of them falls down,
one can help the other up. But pity anyone who
falls and has no one to help them up. Also, if two
lie down together, they will keep warm. But how
can one keep warm alone? Though one may be
overpowered, two can defend themselves. A cord
of three strands is not quickly broken.
ECCLESIASTES 4:9–12 NIV

If you ever needed your friends, it's now! Sure, there's a temptation during the retirement years to pull away from your circle, to rest, relax, and eat, eat, eat. But you can only take that sort of lifestyle for a short time until it gets old.

So, reach out. Do things. Accept invitations. Issue invitations. Have a blast!

Follow Grace's lead. She started small, with a bunko group at her house. That blossomed into a ladies' group that traveled together. They went on cruises, first out of nearby ports and eventually out of ones farther away. They had adventures together she would never have experienced on her own. While on an excursion in Jamaica she met Lydia, a fellow traveler. They hit it off and began to correspond. Before long, they were taking a Mediterranean cruise together.

Sure, it's tempting to pull away, but think of all the things you'll miss if you do! You'll miss fishing trips, cruises, card games, church socials, worship services. You'll miss out on birthday parties, anniversaries, and weddings.

Where's the fun in missing out? No, it's better to get back in the game. You don't have to dive in headfirst, but tiptoe into the pool and then enjoy the experience. And the people. They're pretty great, you know. And they're really hoping you'll say yes the next time they ask.

Lord, I get it. There are plenty of people out there for me to socialize with. Sometimes it's just a matter of actually putting myself in the awkward position of connecting with them. Help me? Please? Amen.

I'll Be Seeing You

*Let us consider how to stir up one another to love
and good works, not neglecting to meet together, as
is the habit of some, but encouraging one another,
and all the more as you see the Day drawing near.*
HEBREWS 10:24–25 ESV

"You'd be perfect for the homeowner's association board, Lisa," Kate said. "Seriously. We need someone with your common sense. And with your background as a CPA you could keep an eye on the finances, too. You have no idea how badly we need that right now. Trust me."

"Well, sure, but . . ." Lisa paced the room as she considered her neighbor's request. "I'm already so active in the seniors' group at church, and James and I just joined that fifty-five-and-up community group . . ."

"All great things. But we could use you too. Pray about it, okay?" Kate gave her a pleading look. "Did I mention you'd be awesome? You really, really would."

Lisa did her best not to sigh aloud and simply responded, "I'll pray about it." It did sound like something she would enjoy, but . . . the buts were adding up right now.

Maybe you understand Lisa's plight. Just about the time you retired, everyone and their brother tried to pull you into their group—their activities. You're struggling to keep up, though you love the interaction with people.

Staying in church is ideal. And participating in other groups can be fun too. There are plenty of clubs to join, places where seniors hang out together. However, keeping life in balance might become an issue if you add too many activities, so pray before you say yes.

And while you're hanging out, don't forget the young people in your life. They still need you too. But again . . . balance. The last thing you need at this point in your journey is the feeling that you're being stretched too thin!

Places to go, people to see, things to do! I want to do it all, Lord! But You'll show me which "things" are mine to take hold of. Guard me from getting overwhelmed, I pray. Amen.

Puppy Love

The righteous care for the needs of their animals,
but the kindest acts of the wicked are cruel.

PROVERBS 12:10 NIV

Alan rolled his eyes as he watched his wife cuddle their cocker spaniel in her lap. "You treat that dog like one of our kids, Missy."

"So what?" Missy glanced his way and shrugged. "She gives me more attention than our grown kids ever do, so why not spoil her a little? Who cares?"

"A little?" He gestured across the room to the dog's expensive bed, which was filled with toys. "You've spent more on Bella than you did on any of the kids. Between the pricey food, the vet, the outfits . . . it's taxing the budget. And don't even get me started on how much that trainer cost. Not that it did any good. She's just as spoiled as she ever was. Maybe more so."

"Don't be silly, Alan. You're exaggerating." She went back to petting her sweet pup, who looked up at her with nothing but pure adoration and love.

"Next thing you know you'll be wanting to convert a bedroom for her. I'll end up taking out a loan to cover the cost, no doubt."

"Never!" Missy gave the lovable pooch a kiss on the forehead. "She sleeps with us, silly. Why would she need her own room?"

"Why, indeed." Alan sighed and went back to reading his book.

Maybe you're like Missy. Your pets have become like your children. They cuddle. They snuggle. They keep you company. And yes, sometimes they even curl up under the covers with you at night. But who cares? God gave you that pup—or kitten or bird or rabbit—as a companion. And you are enjoying their company because it's uncomplicated. Easy. Comfortable. Isn't God so good? He gives us loving, cuddly, furry little creatures to share His love with. And while it's a different type of love than the kind we show our children or our spouses, it's a true connection with a real companion.

*Lord, thank You for placing my pet into my life.
It's another way for me to share Your love with
every being around me, and that brings me
great joy. Amen.*

HOW TO:

Texts to send former coworkers throughout
your day:

1) Have fun at work!

2) Still on my coffee break. (Send at 11 a.m. or
   later.)

3) Just got through golfing. Going to take a nap.
   How's your day going?

4) Headed to a full day at the spa—want to join
   me? Oh! That's right, you have to work! ☺

5) Remember that time we dreamed of not having
   any meetings? My schedule is clear today. Just
   thought you might want to know.

RETHINK

Rethink

Just as each of us has one body with many members, and these members do not all have the same function, so in Christ we, though many, form one body, and each member belongs to all the others.
ROMANS 12:4-5 NIV

We view our lives through a filter shaped by our environment, our friendships, and our families. We do things the way we've been conditioned to do them. Then, as time marches forward, perspectives shift. People change their minds about what they want (or what they thought they wanted). They start to see things differently as their situations morph.

Maybe you're there now. You're rethinking earlier decisions and beginning to dream of a completely different retirement road. It's scary, but you're excited at the same time.

Re-: again
Think: to have a certain (or particular) opinion, idea, or belief about a thing

Maybe you've always done exactly what was expected of you. You played by societal rules and norms. Nothing wrong with that. It's what most of us do, after all. But now you're thinking outside the box. While your friends are making plans to buy an RV or downsize to a condo, you're looking at buying a bigger home on a big patch of land, closer to the grandkids. While they're celebrating days of freedom apart from the daily grind at the office, you're still very much engaged in the work world . . . and you want to keep it that way. In short, you're doing your own thing, marching to your own drumbeat. And that's okay.

Here's the truth: God didn't make you to be a clone of anyone else. If you decide to rethink your retirement years, you will learn to trust Him as never before. And let's be honest: societal norms are often based on customs and traditions that just don't work for you.

Who cares if you're different? Who cares if you take an unusual route? Pleasing those around you isn't what this stage of your life is about, after all. Feeling content with your choices is far more important and will ultimately bring true peace of mind.

Don't worry about how they're doing it. You do you, friend.

I'm rethinking how my retirement years will look, Lord. Guide me and give me peace, I pray. Amen.

Don't Fence Me In

Whatever you do, work at it with all your heart,
as working for the Lord, not for human masters.
COLOSSIANS 3:23 NIV

Just because everyone else is retiring doesn't mean I have to." Randy took another sip of his coffee and leaned back in his chair. Across the table from him, his wife, Cynthia, didn't look convinced.

"But I thought we would travel like our friends are doing. Isn't this the season for all of that?"

"We can still do that, I promise." Randy paused to think through his next words. "I'll cut back my hours at work. But I'm game to keep going as long as they will have me if you're in agreement."

"I . . . I guess." She shrugged and then diverted her gaze to the floor. "I'm just disappointed, I suppose."

"You'd be more disappointed if you were stuck in a house with a man who wasn't quite ready to be here full-time," he responded, choosing his words carefully. If only she could see inside his head and heart right now, she would totally get it. But she couldn't. How could he make her understand? If he left the job now, he would always feel like he'd done the wrong thing. He just wasn't ready yet.

Maybe you feel like Randy. You're not ready to retire. Oh, sure . . . everyone around you is doing it. But in your occupation, you have the option to keep going and you want to. You don't feel led to call it quits just yet.

There's a lot to consider, but just because everyone else is doing something doesn't mean you have to. The number sixty-five isn't stamped in ink, after all. So, think outside the box. And remember the words of comedian George Burns, who said: "Retirement at sixty-five is ridiculous. When I was sixty-five I still had pimples."

Lord, I'm open to whatever You want to do with me at this age and stage of life. Show me where to go and how long to stay there. Amen.

Ain't That a Kick in the Head?

The LORD gave this message to Jonah son of Amittai: "Get up and go to the great city of Nineveh. Announce My judgment against it because I have seen how wicked its people are." But Jonah got up and went in the opposite direction to get away from the LORD. He went down to the port of Joppa, where he found a ship leaving for Tarshish. He bought a ticket and went on board, hoping to escape from the LORD. . . .
JONAH 1:1–3 NLT

George pushed the papers away, overwhelmed. If he hadn't filed for that tax extension, this return would've been turned in months ago. But a health scare back in April meant pushing off the inevitable until he was healthy enough to tackle it. Now he was at the rubber-meets-the-road stage . . . and wishing he could skip town.

Maybe you've struggled through a rough rubber-meets-the-road season recently too. You were forced to look face-first at a tough situation. A financial woe. Estate planning. Caregiving for an elderly parent. Long-term care for a loved one. Or perhaps, like George, the IRS.

Life is hard. And these reality checks can be a kick in the head (and the gut). It's easier to ignore things, to let them go a few months. (Can I get an extension on the hard stuff, Lord? Please?) But facing the inevitable, hard as it might be, is totally doable with God's help. You could run (like Jonah did). But remember, he ended up in the belly of a big fish. That's no place to work out your troubles. No, you need to run straight to God. Get His perspective, His power, His wherewithal to tackle that problem head-on.

No matter what you're facing today, take a deep breath . . . and trust Him with it. Don't let feelings of discouragement or fear stop you from doing the one thing you know you should be doing. Dive in. Get it over with. Then, when this season is behind you, you'll finally be able to draw a deep breath without thinking about it.

I won't run from this, Lord. Instead, I'll dive right in . . . with Your help. Oh, help! Amen.

It's Your Thing

Do not conform to the pattern of this world, but be transformed by the renewing of your mind. Then you will be able to test and approve what God's will is—His good, pleasing and perfect will.
ROMANS 12:2 NIV

Y ou're running a race?" Lucie stared at her friend in amazement.

"Yep." Patti lifted up the pair of sneakers she'd just purchased in anticipation of the event. "It's a 5K. Three months from now. Want to do it with me? I can tell you where to get the perfect running shoes, on sale, no less."

Lucie couldn't help but chuckle at that notion. "Girl, if you ever see me running, someone is probably chasing me. I don't run 5Ks. And I've never known you to run them either."

Patti set the shoes down and shrugged. "Well, I've been working out at the community center and my trainer suggested it."

"You have a trainer?" This was news.

"I do now. Trying to stay in the best possible shape. Just because I'm getting older doesn't mean I have to get flabby."

"Ouch." Lucie tried not to take her friend's words personally. The past few months at home had added a few extra pounds to her midsection after all. But why in the world would Patti feel the need to run a 5K? Who took up running in their sixties? And who bought special shoes for the occasion?

Maybe you're like Lucie's friend Patti. You might be retiring, but you're not ready to slow down. In fact, you see this season as an opportunity to attempt some of the things you've been itching to try. Joining the gym, perhaps. Water aerobics. Joining a quilting group. Traveling. Taking up a new sport like tennis. This is your season and you want to enjoy it, so go for it! Don't let the naysayers keep you from trying new things!

Lord, I love the sense of adventure I'm feeling now that I don't have to work every day. It's so great to have options. I don't want to conform to what everyone else is doing just because I'm in my retirement years. I want to be free to explore the options You're placing in front of me! Amen.

Daydream Believer

I am the vine; you are the branches. Whoever abides
in me and I in him, he it is that bears much fruit, for
apart from me you can do nothing.

JOHN 15:5 ESV

Saundra eased herself up from the sofa, gripping the handles of the walker to brace herself.

"You okay over there, Mom?" Her daughter Nancy looked up from her book and glanced her way. "Need help?"

"I'm fine. Won't be long before I'm back up and running again."

"I'm here in the meantime." Nancy flashed a broad smile. "Where are you headed?"

"I've decided I want to write a book," Saundra explained.

"A book?"

"Mm-hmm. And what better time than now, when my knee is healing. My fingers and brain are still working fine. Besides, I'm getting bored just sitting here. I don't want to let my current limitations define me or keep me from moving forward. That might not make any sense to you, but it's important to me."

"It does make sense, Mom. I'm just surprised that

you're interested in writing a book. I had no idea you were into writing."

"I've spent the past three years of my retirement tracing our family tree back to the 1500s in Scotland. It's been a fascinating journey. And the stories I've learned about our ancestors are remarkable. So, I thought it would be nice to compile them into a book for future generations to enjoy."

"What kind of stories?" Nancy closed her book and rose to take several steps in her mother's direction.

"Like your great-great-grandmother who owned a boardinghouse in a small Texas town. Oh, the stories I could tell you about the folks who came through that place! Let's just say not all of them were stellar folks."

This led to a lengthy conversation between mother and daughter about their family's history. Before long, they were all laughter and smiles.

Maybe you're like Saundra. You've spent your retirement season delving into the world of ancestry and you've got some compelling stories. Now it's time to chronicle those for your children, grandchildren, and future generations. You've got the time. You've got the ambition. Now, get to it! The next generation is counting on you!

I can't wait to get started, Lord! Thanks for loading me up with ideas! Amen.

For Once in My Life

Have I not commanded you? Be strong and courageous. Do not be frightened, and do not be dismayed, for the LORD your God is with you wherever you go.
JOSHUA 1:9 ESV

It's not like I'm jumping out of a plane, sweetheart." Daisy gave her son a pensive look. "I'm just going on a cruise to the Greek isles for three weeks."

"Alone."

"With my friend Donna. She's the same one I went on that three-day road trip with last spring. We love having adventures together."

"Sure, but Greece? Really, Mom? That's on the other side of the world. You'll have to fly there first. Have you thought of that?"

"Well, of course. I already have my tickets. And it's not just the two of us anyway. We're going with a seniors' group, and we even have an experienced tour guide who travels the Mediterranean regularly."

"But . . ."

"But . . . this is a dream come true for me. My whole life I've wanted to travel. I've saved for it, planned for it, prayed about it. Now I finally have the opportunity. Don't try to talk me out of it, Harrison. I'm going, and I'll have the time of my life with Donna and the others."

He muttered something under his breath that sounded like, "If you live through it," but Daisy ignored him. No doubt he was worried about her. This was a bit out of character, after all. But for years she'd dreamed of a trip like this and nothing—and no one—would stop her now that the plans had been set in motion.

Maybe you're facing a similar problem. You've got aspirations to do great things, but there's a worrier in your life. You do your best to squelch the fears, but it's hard. It's time to be brave and daring, friend! Use wisdom, but don't let the fears of others stop you from pursuing the things you feel led to do. Ask God to guide you every step of the way. He will!

Thanks for making me brave, Lord! I'm ready to try new things! Amen.

HOW TO:

Burn calories:

Wriggle, twist, gyrate, and shout. Then, once you've got your bathing suit on, head to the pool.

REALITY

Reality

My mind tells me I'm still young but with each
birthday I know that is not true.
BILLY GRAHAM

You're at that must-face-reality stage in your life. Finances. The reflection in the mirror. Your relationships. Diet. Exercise (or the lack thereof). You've avoided some of those topics for a while now, and it's showing.

Let's take a look at the word reality to see how "keeping it real" can work to your advantage during your retirement years.

Reality: the actual state of things, as they exist, not as you wish them to be.

Many of us tend to take an idealistic view of life. We hope for the best and ignore the signs that things are veering off course until it's too late. (Ever bounce a check or run out of gas? Welcome to the club!)

So, what sort of reality checks have you had to face lately? Financial? Health-, diet-, or exercise-related? Relational? All these things can be hiccups to your plans, bumps in the road, as it were. You don't plan for them, but there they are staring you in the face.

It's time to add a re- to your reality, friend. Give your current situation a closer look. Again. Even if you've done it before. Don't assume the bank account is fine if you're not watching it or working with a budget. Don't assume those friendships are peachy keen if you haven't checked in with your loved ones for a while. Don't assume your blood sugar, cholesterol, and health are on target if you refuse to keep an honest eye on them.

Reality stares you in the face. It's time to stare back . . . and do something about the problem areas. Remember, you will never overcome those things you refuse to see.

So, see them. Work on them. With God's help, your reality can shape up to be shipshape.

I've avoided some of these things long enough, Lord! Give me the courage to face them head-on. I don't want any surprises. No matter how tough my current reality might be, I know I can make it through with Your hand holding mine. Amen.

*Do not rebuke an older man but encourage him
as you would a father, younger men as brothers,
older women as mothers, younger women as
sisters, in all purity.*
I TIMOTHY 5:1-2 ESV

I've been thinking about getting some chickens."

"Wait . . . what?"

Karen smiled as the idea took hold. "Just think about it, Paul. If we had our own chickens, we could have fresh eggs every morning for breakfast. Doesn't that sound yummy? And I would always have eggs for baking. I know how much you love my cookies, pies, and cakes. Oh, and fried chicken! We'd have plenty of that, for sure."

"Well, yes, but who's going to build the pen for these chickens?" He crossed his arms at his chest. "And feed them every day?"

"They don't eat much," she argued.

"But they eat often. And I know you, Karen. You would never let me kill one of those chickens, so the idea that you would fry one up in a pan is a pipe dream."

"You might be right about that."

"Whatever happened to our plans to travel the

globe when we retire? How can we travel if we have chickens?"

"We'll get chicken-sitters."

"Now I'm paying for chicken-sitters?" He groaned and slapped himself on the forehead. "Karen, you've had some crazy ideas, but this one takes the cake."

"Oh, cake! Have I ever told you that I want to open a home bakery? People love my pineapple upside-down cake! That's how I'll use my eggs!"

Maybe you can relate to Karen. You've come up with some ideas that didn't make much sense to others, at least in the moment. Tending to chickens in a suburban home might not be the norm, but it might be doable. Maybe. If the homeowner's association is on board. And your family members. And your neighbors. And the dog.

Hmm. Maybe those chickens weren't your best idea after all. That's okay! Remember, some ideas are just . . . ideas. You're not supposed to carry through with them. So, go ahead. Dream. But before you go out and buy any baby chicks, pray about it and get God's input. Could be He's got something completely different in mind.

I'm such a dreamer, Lord! I'm loaded with ideas—the good, the bad, and the crazy. Help me discern which ones are doable (and beneficial to my situation). Amen.

Sugar, Sugar

God's Word is better than a diamond,
better than a diamond set between emeralds.
You'll like it better than strawberries in spring,
better than red, ripe strawberries.
PSALM 19:10 THE MESSAGE

I never used to have blood sugar issues," Cameron explained. "It started just after I retired. Not sure what happened, honestly."

"Any changes in your diet?" the nutritionist asked as she looked up from her laptop where she had been typing in notes.

"Well, now that you ask . . ." He paused. How much should he tell this gal? She was a total stranger to him. Should he mention that he'd been eating out more since his wife's death? Should he add that he often skipped meals and snacked on chips instead? Should he tell her that living alone without a job to look forward to every day meant more time on his hands to make bad choices?

Nah, he'd skip all that. Instead, he shrugged and said, "I have no idea why my sugars are up. I'm doing the best I can."

Okay, so maybe Cameron wasn't completely

honest about his actions. The truth is he was lonely and a little depressed. And he found himself in a situation that many retirees face—more time for more nibbling.

No matter where you are in the retirement journey, you can always turn to God to give you a peace beyond understanding, an eternal hope, and an unwavering, deep-seated joy. He is the Great Healer, and He loves you. So why not reach out to Him in prayer before trying to eat your feelings away next time? He's there already, and He wants to guide you out of the dark into the light.

Don't give up. Don't give in. Don't worry, friend! God is fighting your battles and working all things out for your good.

I'll do it Your way, Lord! Show me how to get this crazy life of mine under control, I pray. Amen.

Twist and Shout

*Therefore lift your drooping hands and strengthen
your weak knees, and make straight paths for
your feet, so that what is lame may not be put
out of joint but rather be healed.*

HEBREWS 12:12–13 ESV

Well, honey? How did it go at the doctor?"
Fred groaned as he tossed the paperwork
onto the coffee table. He dropped into the recliner
and put his feet up. "Honestly? He's not the nicest
guy in the world. I might be looking for a new doctor
after today, if you want the truth."

"Oh?" Rena looked up from her book to see
why her husband sounded so troubled. "Why is
that?"

"I told him that my back goes out more than I
do, and you won't believe what he said!"

Rena closed her book, looking more than a
little worried. "Not bad news, I hope."

"That crazy fella said, 'I don't need to look at
your X-rays to see what's wrong with your back. I
just need to look at your birthday!'"

Oh boy. Maybe you have walked a mile in
Fred's shoes. You're not a spring chicken anymore.

You've got aches and pains in places that used to feel just fine. You creak. You groan. You're like a bowl of breakfast cereal every time you stand up—snap, crackle, pop. If you can stand up, that is. Some days just getting up off the sofa is a challenge. (Hello, knees! Remember when you used to feel normal? Hey, lower back! You can ease up on me now! I've had enough of this!)

Sure, this part of aging isn't fun, but you've got to keep it in perspective. Remember, strength comes from the inside. Keep building yourself up in the inner man. If the outer one wastes away, then you'll still be able to fall back on the God who lives inside.

I don't like this part of aging, Lord. I really don't. I want every joint, every muscle, every ligament to operate as it should. Show me what I can do to be in the best possible shape. And on those achy days, teach me to lean on You. Amen.

They Can't Take That Away from Me

My people will abide in a peaceful habitation,
in secure dwellings, and in quiet resting places.
ISAIAH 32:18 ESV

"You're moving to a bigger house?"

Mary nodded. "Yes. I know what you're thinking, Carolina. We're seniors. We're supposed to be downsizing. All the cool kids are doing it. But we're thinking that we'd like to have the extra space. Jake and I have found a home in a seniors' community that's just perfect for us. Four bedrooms. A big dining room to have the whole family over for Thanksgiving dinner. We've always had to cram everyone in at our current place. Now we'll have more room to spread out our stuff and let the family come and stay, if they'd like. Best of all, it's in our price range, so we can live there debt-free. It's really ideal for us."

"But . . ." Carolina did not look convinced.

"I know, I know. We're not your typical retirement couple. But this is what works for us, and we're very excited."

"And that's what matters most, of course."

Maybe Mary's words resonate with you. All

your friends are downsizing. They're selling off their valuables, giving away excess furniture, and moving into duplexes or townhomes. Many are shifting to retirement communities with apartment options. They're trading in the macro for the micro. But that's not for you. You don't want to go small; you want to go big.

Good for you! This isn't follow-the-leader, friend! And "normal" is highly overrated, after all. The retirement years aren't a one-size-fits-all proposition. So, you do you. And enjoy it as you do!

Lord, I know that my ideas fly in the face of what most folks my age think and feel. I'm so glad You've freed me up to be myself during this fun season. Amen.

I Fall to Pieces

Give all your worries and cares to God, for He cares about you. Stay alert! Watch out for your great enemy, the devil. He prowls around like a roaring lion, looking for someone to devour. Stand firm against him, and be strong in your faith.

I PETER 5:7–9 NLT

just have that weird, unsettled feeling," Sarah said. "I can't shake it. I retired a year ago, and my heart and mind still don't know what to make of the transition. This season I'm in is so odd."

"How so?" Sarah's daughter Amber gave her mother a pensive look.

"Well, for one thing, I'm anxious . . . a lot. I have trouble falling asleep, and then I have trouble staying asleep. When I wake up, I feel crummy. And I can trace all this back to the change in my lifestyle when my job ended."

"I've been worried about you, Mom. The exhaustion and tension are showing."

"I'm sorry, honey."

"No need to apologize to me. That's not what I mean. I just want things to go back to normal for you."

Sarah sighed. "See? That's the problem. Nothing

is normal right now, and I'm starting to wonder if it ever will be."

Maybe you connect with Sarah on some level. "They" said this would be the best season of your life. Things are supposed to be easy. But instead, you're battling—depression, physical woes, exhaustion, and all sorts of other issues as well. Your "easy" is a lot harder than you'd imagined.

Here's where grace comes in! God has already granted you His grace, but it's time for you to pour out a little on yourself as well. Don't get mad at yourself when things aren't as you'd hoped. Don't beat yourself up on the days when you don't have the energy to get things done.

But by the same stretch, don't be content to live in that valley. Make a plan. Create an exit strategy.

Get back to living—for your sake and those around you. Those unsettled feelings? They're just feelings. They are fleeting. Temporary. Chase after the things that are eternal, and those worries will dissipate.

Lord, I have my secret struggles. No one sees the things I battle in private—emotionally, physically, even financially. I'm so grateful that You see and You care. Lift me out of this valley, I pray. Amen.

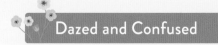

Dazed and Confused

Take no part in the unfruitful works of darkness,
but instead expose them.
EPHESIANS 5:11 ESV

They call it the grandparent scam, and you've got to be so careful not to be taken advantage of!"

"Grandparent scam?" Kathleen looked up from her salad into her daughter's anxious eyes. "What is that, Dani?"

"Usually they send an email or a private message that makes it sound like one of the grandkids is in financial trouble and needs your help." Dani's voice grew more animated as she explained. "Then they talk you into wiring money to help them. Only, it's not really going to a grandchild. It's going to some scammer in another part of the country—or maybe even another part of the world."

"That's terrible!" Kathleen took a sip of her tea as she pondered her daughter's warning.

"Sometimes they call, pretending to be a lawyer. They tell you that your grandchild is in jail and needs thousands for bail."

"I'll be on the lookout, I promise."

"Please do, Mom. And don't ever give your credit

card information to anyone unless you're a hundred percent sure they're legit."

"Well, that's easier said than done," Kathleen responded. "Especially in the internet age! But I'm not really sure why you're worried I'll fall for this particular scam, Dani."

Maybe you've been the victim of a scam. Someone talked you into sharing a credit card number or your checking account information. You felt sure they were the real deal, but they turned out to be skilled manipulators.

The truth is, these folks are predators, and you'll need to keep your eyes wide open. This is the harsh reality of our modern day and age. But you? You're on to them. You won't let yourself be taken advantage of! You've worked too long and too hard to toss your savings away.

Pay attention, friends. Let wisdom lead the way.

Lord, I don't want to be taken advantage of, so I'll keep my eyes open. You've promised to give me wisdom and discernment that gets stronger with age, so I'm leaning on You to guide me. Amen.

HOW TO:

Keep the excitement going when you're out and about:

When the money comes out of the ATM, scream, "I won! I won!"

REENGAGE

Reengage

*Retirement is when you stop living at work
and begin working at living.*
UNKNOWN

You used to be connected with friends, family, and coworkers. You used to get out there and do more. Hang out with people regularly. See the sights. Engage in life's activities. Take trips. But a recent setback forced you to take time off from all of that. You hunkered down, watched a lot of TV . . . put on a few pounds. You got lazy. Bored. Lethargic.

But now you're ready to get rolling again. You want to hit the road, visit people, see all there is to see. You're ready to reengage, to view life through a new filter, to take pictures of the places you've only dreamed of until now.

But what does that look like exactly? Let's break it down.

Re-: again
Engage: to bind, to pledge, to interlock with

For some, reengaging means getting back into relationships with neighbors, friends, and family. For others, it means a road trip to Wisconsin to see your elderly parents. Some people reengage by joining a travel club and taking regular trips with club members. And speaking of trips, some retirees make a big deal out of cruising with friends. (Hey, there's a lot to be said for having your meals made for you and your room cleaned every day!)

No matter how you plan to reengage, it's time! Play bunco with friends. Go to dinner with your daughter. Drive to the country to spend a couple of days in nature. Visit the mountains to reawaken your spirit. Hang out at the beach to ponder God's vastness.

In short, get out there! Hit the road, literally or spiritually. Go beyond the mundane, the everyday, the boring. Engage (interlock—with people, places, and things). Connect (for the sake of your health, your spirit, and your heart). Commit (to a plan, a strategy, a place, or a person).

Do something. Move. Get going.

It's time.

I get it, Lord! It's time! There are places to go, people to see. Life is meant to be lived, and I plan to live it . . . with Your help. What an adventure this season is going to be! Amen.

Papa's Got a Brand New Bag

You will go out in joy and be led forth in peace;
the mountains and hills will burst into song
before you, and all the trees of the field
will clap their hands.
ISAIAH 55:12 NIV

What do you mean, you want to get your pilot's license?" Penny rubbed at her ears, thinking maybe she'd heard wrong. "Chuck, you're sixty-seven years old."

"I know, but I'm not too old to learn."

"To fly a plane?" Penny's heart skipped a beat at the very idea. She knew Chuck routinely ran over curbs when behind the wheel of the car. Now he wanted to lift a metal monstrosity into the air? Surely he had lost his mind. Maybe he wasn't feeling well. He'd been acting a bit strange lately.

"I've always wanted to fly," he explained. "Had a hankerin' to learn years ago. And you know how much I love to travel. I'm always telling you about the trips I want to go on. Well, now we can!"

"Sure, but I never pictured you in the cockpit, that's all. I thought we'd leave that part to a trained pilot."

"I'll be your trained pilot. That's what I'm saying. I'm going to learn to fly."

"Heaven help us." Penny suddenly felt a bit faint.

Maybe you'd feel a little faint thinking about the adventure of learning to fly a plane too. But at your age, it's fun to try new things. And if you're yearning to travel, there are all sorts of ways to get there—by RV, fifth wheel, plane, train, boat, or automobile.

Maybe you won't fly a plane. Maybe you'll rent a boat. Or travel by rail. Or borrow a friend's RV. The point is, you can do something different. Mix it up a bit. Instead of staying at a typical hotel, stay at a bed-and-breakfast. Instead of traveling to see the relatives in Arkansas, have the family meet someplace none of you have ever been before.

It's time to get adventurous, friend!

I'm ready to try something new, Lord!
Let's go! Amen!

Hit the Road Jack

The heart of man plans his way,
but the LORD establishes his steps.
PROVERBS 16:9 ESV

I think they call it wanderlust."

"Wanderlust?" Levi looked up from his laptop where he had been putting together a route for the family's upcoming road trip to Branson, Missouri.

"Yep." His wife read from her phone: "'Wanderlust is the insatiable desire to travel. A person who suffers from this condition isn't content to stay put.'" Shonda gave him a knowing look. "That's you, Levi."

"I guess. There are worse diagnoses, I suppose." He shrugged, then went back to mapping out the trip. They would spend the night in Hot Springs, Arkansas, on the way. And when they arrived in Branson, they would go to the Titanic Museum. The grandkids would love that. Maybe—if it could be arranged—they would all go see The Great Passion Play. He'd heard great things about that.

"There's a cure for wanderlust, I hear." His wife settled into the spot next to him at the kitchen table.

"Oh?" He glanced her way, anxious to get back to his map.

"Mm-hmm." She gave him a kiss on the cheek. "Take two aspirin and invite your wife to join your plans. Ask her to go with you every step of the way. She has wanderlust, too, you know, and wants to be included."

He felt a smile tug up the edges of his lips. Levi slipped his arm around Shonda's shoulders and pulled her close. "For once, I think I'll follow the doctor's orders."

Do you have wanderlust like Levi and Shonda? Do you have a hankering to see the world? Are the mountains calling your name? Do you have an overwhelming desire to watch the ocean waves lap at sandy beaches? If so, then follow the doctor's orders! Hit the road, Jack . . . and don't look back!

I'm ready to hit the road, Lord!

Send Me a Postcard

If I rise on the wings of the dawn, if I settle on the far side of the sea, even there Your hand will guide me, Your right hand will hold me fast.
PSALM 139:9-10 NIV

I'm just trying to figure out how we're going to do this," Arlene said. "If we live six months in Minnesota and six months at the new place in South Texas, who will take care of the Minnesota house while we're away? And what do we do with the plants? Won't they die in the winter without us here to cover them?"

Her husband, Steve, snapped his fingers as if struck with a brilliant idea. "I've got it! Let's offer our place to J.D. from church. He's that young single guy who does web design for some of our families. He works from home, and I happen to remember he's looking for a cheaper place to live."

"I guess if he's self-employed, he could work anywhere," Arlene agreed.

"Yep. He's been struggling to get his business up and running, so if he agrees to stay here and look after things while we're gone, then we won't charge him rent. He can make sure the pipes don't freeze and look after the plants and such."

"And when we leave the Texas house to come back here?" she asked. "Then what?"

"Then we send him to Texas to stay in the house down there. If he's willing. Hey, he's single and not dating anyone at the moment. Maybe he'll think this is the best idea ever."

Can you connect with Arlene and Steve's situation? Do you live in one state part of the year and another state during the other? Are you enjoying the excitement of trying new things in new places? Many retirees live this way. They're called snowbirds because they leave the frigid north during the harsh winters and "fly south" like the birds. Regardless of how you settle down in your retirement years, look for fun and exciting ways to enjoy your home(s) no matter where it or they might be!

Lord, what a fun idea! Living in two places at once? Sounds exciting. Wherever the road takes me, I'm ready for some adventure during this season. Amen.

Like a Rolling Stone

The LORD will keep your going out and your coming in from this time forth and forevermore.

PSALM 121:8 ESV

"Where are we headed today?" Frieda asked as she pulled out the faded map.

"Our favorite RV Park in Ruidoso, New Mexico," her husband responded from behind the wheel of their RV. "Remember it? Nestled right on the edge of a mountain, surrounded by trees. Beautiful place."

"That place? We haven't been there in . . . what's it been? Five years?"

"Closer to six. But I remember it like it was yesterday."

"Six years." Frieda shook her head. "I wonder if Maggie and Kirk still run the place."

"I looked at the website awhile back," Earl said. "They were still listed as the owners. Can't wait to see 'em again."

"Me either. It'll be like old home week." Frieda released a contented sigh. "Ah, Earl, what a blessed life we lead, headed from state to state. We get to enjoy the best of the seasons in some of the finest parks in the country."

"Amen. Love it, honey." He turned to face her. "And I love you. Thanks for pacifying this old man. I always wanted to travel."

"Me too," she responded. "Me too."

Ah, what a life! To hit the road like Frieda and Earl? To see some of the finest places in the country, and at just the right season? Such is the bliss of RV life.

Of course, not every trip is blissful. Vehicles break down. Campsites aren't always perfect. Health issues crop up, gas prices rise, and parking that monstrosity? Not always easy. Oh, but it's all worth it! Think of the friends you'll make along the way and the adventures you'll have! Best of all, you'll get to view God's masterpieces—truly, some of the finest scenery ever—as you go along.

So, what are you waiting for? Pack your bags, make your plans, and grab those keys!

It sounds wonderful, Lord! I can't wait to get started. Show us where to go . . . and when. Amen.

Beyond the Sea

Some went out on the sea in ships; they were merchants on the mighty waters. They saw the works of the LORD, His wonderful deeds in the deep.
PSALM 107:23-24 NIV

Esther stood on board the top deck of the Crystal Seas Voyager and sighed as she looked up at the stars twinkling overhead.

"I know we have these same stars at home," she said to her best friend. "But they don't look like this. Out here they're brighter, more magnificent."

"Not crowded out by city fog, I guess." Joyce leaned against the railing and gazed out at the dark sea, rippling against the motion of the ship as it moved along the waters. "Everything's prettier from the deck of a cruise ship. Have you noticed?"

"Mm-hmm! And that breeze! Have you ever?" Esther held out her arms, as if to take it all in. She wanted this experience to last forever.

They stood in delicious silence with only the sound of the waves to interrupt their thoughts. Joyce's voice finally broke through the stillness. "Hey, I have an idea. Maybe my best yet."

"What's that?" Esther asked, intrigued.

"Ice cream, girl! Free ice cream!"

Esther couldn't help but laugh as she responded, "Yes, please!"

Maybe you've walked—er, traveled—a mile in Esther's shoes. You've been fortunate enough to take a trip on the open seas. There, in that wide expanse of God's neverland, you were free to revel in His vastness, His greatness, His marvelous creation. Under a cloudless, nighttime sky you experienced His wonder all over again, and it touched your soul in a deep and profound way.

Many retirees live for moments such as this. Oh, others might regard their journeys as frivolous, but the travelers know better. Here, away from the mundane, they truly come alive—in their senses, their imaginations, and their relationships. And best of all, they don't have to cook or clean for several glorious days. And (bonus!) . . . free ice cream!

Lord, that sounds wonderful! I want to experience Your vastness—whether it's on the open seas or in my own backyard. May I never stop gazing upward to those beautiful star-filled night skies! Amen.

HOW TO:

Guess a retiree's age:

Ask him if he's the original owner of his '38 Studebaker.

RELAX

Relax

Retirement is wonderful. It's doing nothing
without worrying about getting caught at it.
ANONYMOUS

Ahhh! That moment when you're finally able to relax! All your cares drift away on the wind as you settle down—your heart, your body, and your mind finally at ease. Anxieties fade, tension releases, and you're free at last.

Re-: again
Lax: loose, relaxed, the opposite of tense

Your retirement years are filled with opportunities for relaxation and reflection. But some folks get so wound up with their on-the-go lifestyles that they actually forget to rest. Road trips turn into exhausting, agonizing, problem-filled trials. (Ever have to come home from a vacation to get some rest?) Home improvement projects send you reeling. And relational drama zaps your time and energy. Many times, whole days pass and you realize you didn't take a moment for yourself. (Hey, wasn't that the point of retirement, anyway?)

When you don't take the time to relax, you

can't be refreshed. You don't have time to press the pause button. And God is keen on you taking care of yourself in this way. Don't believe it? Check out this verse: "And he said to them, 'Come away by yourselves to a desolate place and rest a while.' For many were coming and going, and they had no leisure even to eat" (Mark 6:31 ESV).

Jesus called His disciples to "come away" and take a breather. When you take the time to relax, when you deliberately let go of the tensions and take a moment to actually breathe, your body begins to recover. Skip that relaxation and you'll stay wound up tighter than a kite string.

Sure, not everyone knows how to relax. You might fall into that category. But you've got plenty of time to learn now that the retirement years are here. So, kick back. Put those feet up. Let those tensions go, friend!

I'll do it, Lord! I'll let the tensions go. They weren't doing me much good anyway. Teach me how to relax so that my body, heart, and mind can stay healthy and strong, I pray. Amen.

It Is Well with My Soul

Not that I was ever in need, for I have learned how to be content with whatever I have.
PHILIPPIANS 4:11 NLT

Do you ever feel like God's plans for your life ended the day your kids got married?" Tonya asked. "Or when you retired?"

Her counselor leaned forward in her chair. "Could you elaborate on that question? Maybe go a little deeper?"

Tonya shrugged. "When the kids moved away, my reason for being was gone. I was the one who held things together. I was . . ."

"The glue?"

"Yes. Then they moved away and I struggled. But the real kicker came when I retired a few months back."

"That's a hard transition."

"Yes! I couldn't figure out my life plan anymore. I always took care of things—for the kids, for my boss, for my husband. Now he's busy playing golf and I'm home alone, feeling . . ."

"Like God's done with you?" her counselor asked.

"It sounds terrible, hearing it spoken like that," Tonya acknowledged. "But I have to confess, I've felt that way at times. It's almost as if my days of usability are behind me now and He's passed the baton to someone else who's younger, healthier, more . . ."

"More what?"

"Better equipped?" she tried. "I don't know. I just feel like my best days are behind me now."

Maybe you've walked a mile in Tonya's shoes. You're feeling like your best days are behind you too. Like God has passed the proverbial baton from your generation to the next. But here's a wonderful truth: He's got big things for you during this season. He wants to revive your soul (your heart, mind, and strength) so that you can look at your current situation—yes, even the icky one staring you in the face right now—and say "It is well with my soul."

It will be. It can be . . . if you give it to Him.

Lord, I have to confess, it hasn't been well with my soul. It's been anything but. Today I choose to say, "It is well," not because of how I'm feeling, but because I know I can trust You. Amen.

The Sound of Silence

"Be still, and know that I am God. I will be exalted
among the nations, I will be exalted in the earth!"
PSALM 46:10 ESV

"Do you hear that?"

"Hear what?" Isabel asked as she looked around their living room.

"Exactly." Bradley smiled as he drew in a deep breath. "Total and complete silence. Isn't it amazing?"

She laughed. "And here I was just thinking that I'm about to lose my mind because it's so quiet. I was about to turn on some music so I wouldn't go stir-crazy."

"No. Please don't." He lifted his hands as if to emphasize his point. "I'm enjoying this too much. It's a luxury."

"Really? Not me." She laughed. "I can actually hear my heart beating in my ears. And did you notice the car that just drove by? Pretty sure I heard their radio thumping."

"I didn't notice any of that." Bradley offered a shrug. "But after years in my crazy office, the silence is perfect. I consider it a gift."

Maybe you can relate. The kids are grown. The chaos of your office turmoil is behind you. Right now, the dogs aren't even barking. There's no delivery truck at your door, no yard guys mowing the lawn, and no neighbor dogs yap-yap-yapping. In short, it's bliss.

And yet . . . it's different. It's taking some getting used to. You haven't acclimated to your new normal yet and are starting to wonder if you ever will. (Hey, some folks keep the TV going all day just to hear human voices! Ever been there?)

Every new season requires an adjustment period. Whether you're in a crazy-loud household or one that allows you to hear the hum of the AC, you can adapt. You can adjust. You can learn to appreciate your new normal.

No, really.

Lord, show me how to adapt to the volume level in my house. I want to be at peace in my own home. I know I can, with Your help. Amen.

Sittin' on the Dock of the Bay

Simon Peter said to them, "I am going fishing."
They said to him, "We will go with you."
They went out and got into the boat, but that
night they caught nothing.
JOHN 21:3 ESV

"I've always loved to fish," Pete explained. "From the time I was a kid. It was a great escape, a place to get away from things and just . . . be."

His friend Chip smiled. "I understand, trust me. And there's something to be said for bringing home the bacon. Er . . . bass."

"True." Pete paused to think it through. "I love that part, but mostly I just enjoy the quiet time. It's crazy, the things that go through my mind when I've got a fishing pole in my hand. It's almost like God starts talking the minute I settle down."

"Maybe you're just finally quiet enough to hear Him," Chip suggested.

"Could be." He reached for his pole and dropped it into the back of his truck, then grabbed the tackle box. "There's something about it, though. Can't quite put my finger on it. Fishing seems like a holy experience to me."

Maybe Pete had a point. There is something rather holy about getting away from the chaos of life and dropping a line into the water. It's not the act of catching the fish, though that's nice too. It has more to do with the fact that you're rooted and grounded in that spot until you've reached the desired outcome. You're not budging.

Where better to spend time talking to Jesus? Where better to give your troubles to Him? Perhaps, as you toss that line into the water, you can release your cares along with it.

Lord, thank You for giving me "away" time to
rest and relax in Your presence. I love it so much.
Amen.

Tossin' and Turnin'

*I consider that our present sufferings
are not worth comparing with the glory
that will be revealed in us.*

ROMANS 8:18 NIV

Sally stretched her aching feet in the warm,
bubbly water and then watched as the gal doing
her pedicure went to work. She turned to face her
friend Carol, who sat in the chair next to her.

"You know, I remember when I was in my
twenties my dad called me one day and said, 'It's all
downhill after you turn forty.'"

"Boy, he wasn't kidding, was he? Seems like
everything hurts these days."

"I had to buy new glasses," Sally said. "Bifocals.
And don't even get me started on all the doctor visits.
Endocrinologist. Rheumatologist. Neurologist. I see
all the -ologists now."

"Me too, girl. Me too." Carol's nose wrinkled.
"And it seems like every conversation I have with a
friend these days involves one of two topics—joint
pain or bowels."

They had a good chuckle at that one.

No doubt you're able to relate. As we age, our

bodies don't always cooperate! That doesn't mean we have to stop though. We can always work at being our best possible selves.

God gave you that wonderful body to keep! Instead of grumbling about all the things you can't do, take time to think of the things you can do . . . and then do them!

Lord, thank You for this body! It ain't what it used to be, but it's mine. Show me how to be the best possible version of myself! Amen.

Seasons in the Sun

And let us not grow weary of doing good, for in
due season we will reap, if we do not give up.
GALATIANS 6:9 ESV

I t's all about the seasons, isn't it?" Darla leaned
back in her easy chair and took a sip of her coffee.

"I guess you're right." Her sister looked up from
the afghan she was crocheting. "I used to mourn the
fact that my kids were grown and halfway across the
country. These days I just thank God that they're
healthy, employed, and raising good kids of their
own."

"True, that." Darla paused to think it through.
"Mourning the past is highly overrated anyway. It
does no good to go backward. This, I've learned . . .
the hard way."

"Me too." Sadie went back to her crochet work
but kept talking. "And honestly? I'm enjoying this
season I'm in. Things are quieter, but I'm finding
that I'm acclimating well. I enjoy my house, my time
to myself, and my new hobbies. And all my fretting
over being stuck in the house with Ralph 24/7 was
for nothing. He's out fishing or hunting so much of
the time that I actually appreciate him more when
he's around. That helps."

"Perspective." Darla took another sip of her coffee as the word sank in. "That's what the seasons are all about."

"Yep. And I'm glad for it," Sadie agreed.

Perspective is everything, isn't it? God gives us what we need when we need it. He knows the seasons we're going through and has provided the psychological, emotional, and financial help to see us through. Learning to settle into the season is key. It is possible. (Hey, bucking the seasons can lead to nothing but discontentment and pain.)

What season are you in today? Give it to God and watch Him move in your heart and give you all the perspective you need to get through it with joy and grace.

I won't fight the seasons, Lord. I'll lean in to them to hear Your voice and discover Your will for my life. Amen.

HOW TO:

Retirement NOT To-Do List

X Set Alarm

X Get Dressed

X Drive to Work

X Care What Others Think

X Reply to Emails

X Know What Time It Is

X Know What Day It Is

REDO

Redo

Do not lie to each other, since you have taken off
your old self with its practices and have put on the
new self, which is being renewed in knowledge in
the image of its Creator.
COLOSSIANS 3:9–10 NIV

Second chances. Don't you love them? God's in the business of giving His kids opportunities to get things right the second time around. And the third. And the fourth. And so on! There's no better time than during your retirement years to press the "redo button" on several areas of your life.

Re-: again
Do: to bring to pass

Maybe you set goals for yourself but never met them. You aspired to do certain things, had deep desires to accomplish specific goals. You had hoped they would come to pass, but (as of yet) they have not. Here's the truth: there's still time. No, really! There's still time to turn things around. And if you've made mistakes in the past that led to rough outcomes (for yourself or others), there's still time to make those things right too. In fact, God longs for you to make them right and will give you all you need to aid in that process.

Second chances give us hope. They keep us going instead of allowing us to curl up in a ball. Have a relationship that needs rebuilding? It's not too late. Finances in trouble? There's still time for a redo. Need to finally tackle that mess of a house? You can do it, friend.

What areas do you need to take care of today? Maybe it's time to make a list. Then, instead of beating yourself up over how many things you need to fix, give them to God. Ask for His plan, His strategies. And while you're at it, focus on these specific words from today's Scripture passage: "Since you have taken off your old self with its practices and have put on the new self, which is being renewed in knowledge in the image of its Creator" (Colossians 3:10 NIV).

God anticipated our need for redos. He knew that the old self would get in the way, and He has made provision for second (and third and fourth) chances by encouraging us to put on the "new self."

It's not too late. Period.

I'm grateful for the reminder that second chances are still mine for the taking, Lord! Amen.

The Good, the Bad, and the Ugly

Love is patient and kind. Love is not jealous or boastful or proud or rude. It does not demand its own way. It is not irritable, and it keeps no record of being wronged. It does not rejoice about injustice but rejoices whenever the truth wins out. Love never gives up, never loses faith, is always hopeful, and endures through every circumstance.

I CORINTHIANS 13:4-7 NLT

It just seems impossible to me." Mindy swiped at her eyes with the back of her hand. "Our two grown sons act like teenagers sometimes, Paul. They make family gatherings ridiculously hard."

"I know. I agree."

She reached for a tissue and used it to dab her nose, which had taken to running now that the tears had started. "I wish they could just get along. To be honest, I'm fed up with both of them. That's a terrible thing for a mother to say, isn't it? But that's how I feel right now."

Paul rested his hand on his wife's arm. "Don't give up, Mindy."

"I'm close to that point. I'm already dreading Thanksgiving. How awful is that?"

"Typical, in today's society. People can be so . . ."

"Rude?" Mindy groaned. "I just never thought I'd be one of those moms whose grown kids squabble like toddlers."

"Me either, but we've got to keep praying, keep believing, and keep hoping for a positive outcome. That's what I'm doing anyway."

Maybe you've walked a mile in Mindy's shoes. Someone or a group of someones in your world can't seem to get along. They bicker. They argue. They make family gatherings tough. And you're at the jumping off point. Why keep trying to bring the whole family together if they insist on acting like this?

Instead of giving up, use this special season of your life to engage your heavenly Father in intense prayer for this situation. If you stop praying, who will stand in the gap for your loved ones? It's your right, your calling, and a holy privilege.

Okay, Lord . . . I get it. I won't give up on them. I want to. I'm exhausted with their antics. But if You could put up with me all this time, I suppose I can devote more time in prayer for the ones I love too.
Amen.

These Boots Are Made for Walkin'

Gracious words are like a honeycomb,
sweetness to the soul and health to the body.
PROVERBS 16:24 ESV

"Fido has put on three pounds since he was here last time." The vet looked through the dog's paperwork, a concerned look on his face. "Short of a thyroid problem, we might want to look at changing up his diet."

"Oh?" Janet flinched as she realized she was likely to blame for the pooch's paunchy midsection. These past few months she'd been a little lax in walking him. And, because he was bored lounging around the house, he'd been begging for more food. To pacify him, she'd overindulged the poor guy. And now there was a price to pay.

The dog wasn't the only one struggling, she had to admit. Since she'd stopped her daily walks, her muscle tone wasn't quite what it used to be. She missed the youthful enthusiasm she used to feel after those brisk walks in the early morning hours and the leisurely strolls as the sun was going down. These days, she spent far too much time in front of the TV and not enough soaking in the sunshine.

Maybe Fido's problem was her problem too. Perhaps it was time to get both of them moving again. She had the time. She had the desire. All she lacked was the energy. But one thing Janet had learned over the years—a body in motion tends to stay in motion. A body that lounges on the sofa? Well, it tends to stay there until something (or someone) moves it.

"Okay, doc, you've got a point," she said after thinking it through. "Fido and I will both get back to work."

Lord, I have to admit I get a little lazy sometimes. But I don't want my laziness to become a habit. It's one thing to rest; it's another thing to give up on my health routine. Give me the energy, I pray, so that I can get back to it. I need a redo in this area of my life! Amen.

Happy Together

Love is patient and kind; love does not envy or boast; it is not arrogant or rude. It does not insist on its own way; it is not irritable or resentful; it does not rejoice at wrongdoing, but rejoices with the truth. Love bears all things, believes all things, hopes all things, endures all things.

I CORINTHIANS 13:4–7 ESV

She's never going to speak to me again." Sally leaned forward and put her elbows on the table. "I messed up big-time. I don't blame her really."

"Mom, Norma is your best friend. For as long as I can remember, it's been Sally and Norma doing everything together."

"Which makes this falling out ten thousand times worse," Sally confessed. "She's the one I go to with everything. But I really broke her trust. It's on me. I tried to make it right, but she's not ready to forgive me. I wonder if she ever will be."

"Someone very wise once told me there are twelve words to heal any relationship," her daughter said. "I am sorry. I was wrong. Please forgive me. I love you."

Sally's eyes flooded with tears as her daughter

quoted back the line she had used dozens of times over the years.

"If it worked for me, it'll work for you, Mom." Her daughter patted her hand. "How many of those words have you spoken to Norma?"

"Three?" Sally said. "No, actually . . . six."

"Well then, you have six more to go. At least put them out there, Mom. You can't control her reaction, but at least you will have made every effort. And keep trusting God. He's pretty good at putting broken things back together, you know." She offered a little wink. "Someone wise once told me that too."

Wise words, right? God is in the restoration business and wants to offer you a redo for some of your broken relationships. It starts with those twelve words. Who do you need to speak them to?

Lord, today I will humble myself and approach the one I've hurt. Thank You for offering me a second chance. Soften my loved one's heart so that they will offer me one as well, I pray. Amen.

If I Were a Rich Man

Dishonest money dwindles away, but whoever gathers money little by little makes it grow.
PROVERBS 13:11 NIV

It just feels impossible." Corinne groaned and shoved the papers across the table. "I've looked at these bills a hundred different times and in a hundred different ways. But there's more month than money. I can't possibly pay off all this debt. I'm getting nowhere with it and feel hopeless."

"Then maybe it's time for a debt consolidation loan, Mom," her daughter suggested. "Lots of folks go through that. Or they hire a debt resolution company to help them pay off their bills at lower rates. There are services like that out there."

"I guess."

"What have you done so far?"

Corinne shrugged. "Since your dad died, I've just been paying the minimum on all these credit cards. But the balances are going up every month and it's overwhelming."

"Then it's time to turn things around. But first, we pray." Her daughter reached for her hand, and before she knew what hit her, that precious woman of God was praying the house down, asking for God's direction, mercy, and heavenly intervention.

Maybe you're in Corinne's shoes right now. The financial woes are overwhelming. It seems impossible. Remember, God delights in doing the impossible! It might sound cliché to say, "Give it to Jesus," but if you're holding too tightly to something, you're not fully trusting God to work on your behalf.

So, give it to Jesus. No, really. Today. Right now. Lift your hands, your heart, and your problem before His throne and give it to Him once and for all.

I know I can trust You, Lord. Thank You for offering redos, even on something as complicated as my bills! Amen.

Memories Are Made of This

But the Advocate, the Holy Spirit, whom the
Father will send in My name, will teach you
all things and will remind you of everything
I have said to you.
JOHN 14:26 NIV

Would you say we're hoarders, Robert?" Mazie looked around her cluttered living room and sighed. "Because I'm starting to think there's no other word for it."

He glanced up from his newspaper and looked around. "We have a lot of stuff, but there's plenty of room to get around. I think hoarders have a bigger mess than this." His gaze shifted back to the newspaper.

Mazie wasn't so sure. They seemed to have an excessive amount of stuff—some of it important and some not. Every room was filled with precious and priceless memories, everything from cards the grandkids had made to photos of trips they'd taken in the 1980s.

Lately, Mazie had started to feel overwhelmed by it all. Instead of enjoying those memories, she found the rooms hard to keep clean. Dust bunnies set up camp on every picture frame and knickknack.

"I've been watching those home organizing shows," she explained. "And they say that less is more. Don't you think we should start to purge and only leave out the things that really matter to us? Maybe the items we put on display will have more meaning if there aren't so many of them vying for our attention."

"Maybe." He closed the paper. "So, when do you want to do this?"

She leaned forward in her chair, suddenly filled with zeal for the task. "Might sound crazy, but I say we dive right in."

Maybe you're where Mazie is. You're tired of the clutter. You can't enjoy any of your items because you're so overwhelmed by them. Today is the perfect day to begin the organizational process. Before long, your home will be clean, organized, and beautifully adorned with the things that matter most—if you'll go ahead and get that ball rolling now.

I'll stop putting it off, Lord! I'm ready to begin the task of getting things in order, but I'll definitely need Your help. Amen.

HOW TO:

Change the oil in your vehicle:

Buy a car. Get in your car. Drive to the mechanic's shop.

REDEDICATE

Rededicate

Each of you should use whatever gift you have
received to serve others, as faithful stewards of
God's grace in its various forms.
I PETER 4:10 NIV

A retiree will never be lonely as long as he's found a place of service. Have you ever thought about all the fun and exciting ways to use your gifts and abilities at your local church?

Many churchgoers get involved in food pantries, mission projects, church-planting programs, and a host of other outreach endeavors. This could be the perfect season to see where God will take you, ministry-wise, because you've likely got more time on your hands. But it all begins with one very important word:

Re-: again
Dedicate: consecrate, set yourself apart, commit
to a particular action, devote

Is it time to rededicate yourself to your local church? If so, what does that look like for you? Start by answering this simple question: Do you sense a calling to serve in a particular area? Have you been itching to work in the nursery? Volunteer at VBS? Mentor young moms? Lead a men's Bible study? Help take care of the church property? Serve at the women's events? Sing in the choir? Work in media arts? Direct traffic? Clean up after service? Great! Dive in! Whether you're interested in singing, serving, or scrubbing, there's plenty to keep you busy. (And who knows . . . you might just inspire others to do the same!)

Wherever you are in your journey, this could be the perfect time to minister to others. And think of all the friends you'll make! After all, there are retirees aplenty at your local church, and most are looking for ways to hang out together. Serving alongside each other will bless you and others.

Lord, would You like me to serve at the church? I want to be a blessing to others but I'm not sure how to do it. Show me where my gifts and abilities can best be utilized. Amen.

That Lucky Old Sun

*For length of days and years of life and
peace they will add to you.*
PROVERBS 3:2 ESV

Do you think we take life for granted?" Marilyn
asked.

Her neighbor Coral glanced her way before
easing down into her new leather recliner. "How so?"

"I mean, we plod along, treating life as a mundane
thing. Every day feels a bit like the one before it.
We treat everything as if it's . . . ordinary." Marilyn
sighed. "But it's not! Sometimes I think we forget
to marvel in the blessings that God pours out on us
every single day—brilliant sunsets, puppies' kisses,
morning dew on the grass, the smell of the flowers in
the garden. These are all marvelous gifts that we take
for granted."

"Hey, speak for yourself!" Coral leaned back
in her recliner and kicked up her feet. "I live every
day to the fullest. Like right now, for instance. I'm
pausing to thank the Lord for this amazing chair He's
given me to elevate these puffy feet. It's a modern-
day marvel, this electric chair of mine. I don't take it
for granted."

Marilyn laughed. "Okay, okay. I see your point. I just don't want to miss what's right in front of me. We're so blessed to have each and every day."

"Especially when we can put our feet up."

Perhaps both ladies had it right! Life is a gift, isn't it? And it's filled with precious things to enjoy, offerings from our generous Creator, who made everything for our enjoyment. Of course sometimes, as Marilyn said, we plod along, forgetting to marvel at the brilliance of each new day.

But no more! Today is the perfect day to pause and thank God for giving you another opportunity to live, to love, and to celebrate His goodness. What a blessing, to have another day to live for Him!

Lord, may I never forget that each day is filled with wonder! Open my eyes to all You've given me. May I have a grateful heart for every single gift. Thank You for each new day. Amen.

My Generation

*They devoted themselves to the apostles'
teaching and to fellowship, to the breaking of
bread and to prayer.*

ACTS 2:42 NIV

"We're going on a field trip this Tuesday, and we'd love it if you could join us."

Stacey shifted the phone to her other ear as she contemplated her friend's words. "I'm so busy around the house, Lucy. I'm sorting through all those boxes in the garage and getting ready for that big neighborhood garage sale next month."

"You can't take a break from that to join us?" Lucy's voice now had a bit of a pout. "We're going to have so much fun! And I remember how much you used to love doing these trips with us before Carlton died. You were the life of the party."

"Yeah." She sighed as she surveyed the messy garage. "That was then; this is now. My situation has changed."

"But your need for socialization and fellowship hasn't," Lucy reminded her. "Just think about it, okay? It's good to be with people in your age group. We can relate to what you're going through. And remember, there's strength in numbers. We'll be your arm lifters, if you let us."

Maybe you're like Stacey. You've decided it's too much trouble to "join the group." Let them have their field trips. Let them have their Taco Tuesdays at the church. They won't understand what you're going through right now.

Only, what if they do? What if that group is the answer to the loneliness you've been facing? What if these retirement years weren't meant to be handled completely by yourself, tackling problems with no help? What if those friends could come and help you organize the garage?

Something to think and pray about, friend.

Lord, sometimes it's easier not to belong. I stick to myself, do my own thing. I see others getting together, taking trips, having fun, but I'm just not there yet. Help me make the transition, I pray. I know my life would be more fun with people in it! Amen.

Stop and Smell the Roses

*He said to them, "Come away by yourselves
to a desolate place and rest a while."
For many were coming and going, and
they had no leisure even to eat.*
MARK 6:31 ESV

"For forty years I worked in a fast-paced environment," Patrick explained. "Every single day was like a race. I burned calories—and brain cells—from sunup to sundown. Now I want to do the opposite. I'm ready to just . . ."

"Stop and smell the roses?" his wife, Maggie, asked.

"Exactly." He paused to think through his next words. "I just feel like I missed so much when I was working at the refinery. Life was marching on around me, but I didn't get to participate. From inside the walls of the building I missed the changing of seasons and church events. I even missed watching the kids take their first steps."

"I remember."

"I didn't get to see Sadie all dressed up for her first dance, remember?"

"I do."

"And when Jimmy passed his driving test? I was working that day."

"Aw, Patrick. This is really hitting you hard, isn't it?"

"It is. But, no more. I want to be there for the grands and great-grands. And I want to get outdoors more and take in more of nature. Are you game?"

Maggie's face lit into a smile. "Am I ever! You wouldn't believe how long I've waited to hear you speak those words, in fact!"

Maybe you're like Patrick. You've spent years working hard for the company. You missed a lot. More than you'd realized. Now you finally have an opportunity to participate in life, and you don't want to miss a thing! A child's smile. That first tooth. The hummingbirds in your backyard. That gorgeous sunset. It's all yours for the taking. You're ready to push aside distractions and settle your heart and spirit. Perhaps your greatest plan is no plan at all. It's simply . . . to be.

Lord, I want to stop and smell the roses. I've marched right by them for years, missing out on so much. But no more! Show me how to settle in and actually enjoy the time You've given me. Amen.

All You Need Is Love

As each has received a gift, use it to serve one another, as good stewards of God's varied grace.
1 PETER 4:10 ESV

I just want to feel useful," Mark said. "Doesn't matter where. Doesn't matter when. I'm not picky. Put me in the parking lot and I'll guide the congregation in. Or put me at the front door. I'll be happy to be a greeter. Whatever you think, Pastor."

Maybe you have the same desire to serve. Like Mark, you're not picky. If they need help making coffee, you'll make coffee. If they want someone to serve up cookies at VBS, you're okay with that. If they need a mechanic to change oil for single moms, you're in. If they want someone to mow the church's lawn, you're ready to pull out that riding lawnmower. You've got a heart that's ready to serve, and it's not about you . . . it's about them.

God loves a servant's heart. And yes, He can use you even now. Age doesn't limit you from usability. Or serve-ability. The need is great and you've got passion. That's all that's needed in many cases.

So, make the offer. But don't be surprised if the

church falls so in love with your big heart that they use you again and again.

Here's a fun fact based on today's Scripture: You've received gifts (like the gift of gab, for instance). Use it to encourage others. You've been given other gifts (like organization, for instance). Use it to help in the church's food pantry.

You get the point. All those gifts that you take for granted? They can all serve a purpose in your local church. So, if you're called to serve, start by analyzing your strengths, then find your perfect fit. Before long you'll be bouncing from area to area, a happy, joyous servant, making a difference for the kingdom of God.

Thanks for using me, Lord! I know that I have natural gifts and abilities, but I haven't really considered the fact that they make me usable in my church. If you want me to spend my time and energy at church, show me how and where I fit so that I can have the biggest impact, I pray. Amen.

Don't Take Away the Music

Let the message of Christ dwell among you
richly as you teach and admonish one another
with all wisdom through psalms, hymns,
and songs from the Spirit, singing to God
with gratitude in your hearts.
COLOSSIANS 3:16 NIV

Pete, you should join the community theater guild."

"The theater guild?" Pete stared at the play director, stymied by his request. "I've been at this community for thirty years and have never acted a lick, Jay. You know that."

"But Gloria tells me you used to." Jay gave him a knowing look. "It's like riding a bicycle. It'll come back to you if you try."

"I'm not so sure about that." The whole idea sounded ludicrous. "I don't even perform for my family anymore."

"Just pray about it. We could use more men in our next musical, especially baritones."

"What makes you think I'm a baritone?" Pete asked, now more than a little curious.

"I can tell by your speaking voice. Well, at least

I think I can." Jay grinned. "Why don't you come by the theater and let me listen to your range. Just a few warm-ups and we'll both have our answer."

"W–what? Now?"

Maybe you've been in Pete's shoes. You used to act. Or sing. Or play an instrument. Those things came naturally to you. They were a part of who you were and how you interacted with others.

Now you're faced with the possibility of reawakening that old gift and bringing it to the surface again so that you can be a blessing once more. There's no time like the present! Hey, nothing is outside the realm of possibility as long as you're willing!

The point is, God gave you those gifts for a reason. He wants you to use them, not let them lie dormant. So, what's keeping you? Grab those tap shoes and get busy!

Lord, it's been so long, I don't even know if I can anymore. But I trust You to help me as I try. Amen.

HOW TO:

Get over peer pressure:

Live to be 104.

REVIVE

Revive

*He has made everything beautiful
in its time. He has also set eternity in the human
heart; yet no one can fathom what God has done
from beginning to end.*
ECCLESIASTES 3:11 NIV

When you think of the word revive, what comes to mind? Perhaps you've been to an old-time revival where the evangelist gave a rousing sermon followed by a passionate plea for folks to come forward to the altar. Or maybe you've experienced personal revival in your soul—an encounter with God so deep, so personal, that it shook you to the core and set your feet on a path toward spiritual healing. Let's take a look at the definition of revival.

Revive: to bring back to life, resuscitate,
to give spirit to

Don't you just love that image of "giving spirit" to something? That's what God wants for you during this season of your life. He wants to fully revive you, to draw you closer to Himself than you've ever been before. He wants to bring your spirit-man back to life (raise him from the dead), resuscitate you so that you're fully alive in Him and ready to do great things for the kingdom. If there was ever a time to give yourself fully to Him, it's now.

Here's a fun side note: God never really had a retirement plan for you. It's true! Retirement isn't necessarily a biblical principle. The Bible doesn't touch on things like Medicare, Social Security, or a retirement account. In fact, God plans for you to keep going . . . forever.

That's right. He's got an eternal plan in mind for you. Instead of slowing down, He wants you to continue to build yourself up in the inner man, to get excited about spending eternity with Him.

Where are you in your spiritual walk, friend? Just because your outer man is growing weaker doesn't mean the inner you has to do the same. (Hey, think of all the biblical greats who did amazing things for God in their later years!)

You can be fully alive in Him no matter your age. Today, make a commitment to draw close . . . closer than ever before.

I give myself to You afresh, Lord! Make the rest of my days the best of my days as I come alive by Your Spirit! Amen.

Till the End of Time

He has made everything beautiful in its time. Also,
he has put eternity into man's heart, yet so that he
cannot find out what God has done from the
beginning to the end.
ECCLESIASTES 3:11 ESV

Have you ever stopped to think about forever?" Gina asked her granddaughter.

Nine-year-old Jenna shook her head.

"When we get to heaven, we're going to live forever . . . and ever . . . and ever."

"A hundred billion years?" Jenna asked.

"Longer!" Gina explained, her excitement mounting. "There's no such thing as time in heaven, honey."

"No time?"

"Nope! No clocks at all! Only . . . forever and ever with Jesus, the one who created you and loves you more than life itself! Doesn't that sound amazing?"

Jenna's eyes sparkled with excitement at the prospect. "I can't wait!"

"Oh, that's the best part." Gina reached over to give her granddaughter's hand a squeeze. "You don't have to. Eternity can start today if you ask Jesus to come and live in your heart!"

"Yes, please!" Jenna nodded, eyes wide. "Thank you, Grandma!"

Maybe you're like Jenna. You haven't fully understood the concept of eternity. "Forever and ever" seems like a mighty long time, but there's nothing time-related about it! You'll spend eternity basking in the glow of the One who adores you! (Hey, let's face it: When you were young and in love, you didn't pay any attention to the clock. You were simply content to "be" with the one you adored. Right?)

That's what heaven will be like. Toss those clocks. Get rid of those preconceived ideas. Settle in next to your Creator, and marvel at His deep, abiding love for you, His child. And in the meantime, begin to have an eternal perspective. Don't look at your current troubles through an earthly veil, a limited timeline. Begin to view them in light of eternity. There! Doesn't that put them in perspective?

I get it, Lord! You don't want me to get so caught up in the worries and woes of this life that I lose my eternal perspective. You placed eternity in my heart for a reason! I want to begin to enjoy it right here and right now. Bless You for that. Amen.

One Day at a Time

So don't worry about tomorrow, for tomorrow will bring its own worries. Today's trouble is enough for today.
MATTHEW 6:34 NLT

It's one thing to talk about living in the present, it's another thing to live it out! Annie found out the hard way after she retired and waited on news about a new project, a writing assignment for a local paper. Would they like her work? Would they offer her a part-time freelance position? An occasional local piece, perhaps? She had prayed about it, sought the Lord's will, and sent in samples of her work. Now, to wait. Only, she didn't do that very well.

Days went by and she didn't hear anything. By the time the news came, she had almost convinced herself the editor hated her work. Turned out, he loved it! In fact, he loved it so much that he offered her a weekly column of her very own.

Maybe you're like Annie. You don't wait well. You anticipate the worst. You want Him to move . . . now. Not tomorrow. Not the day after that. And certainly not the week or the month after. You're anxious. You're ready. Only, He's making you hang on a bit longer.

The prescription for waiting can be found in today's verse: "So don't worry about tomorrow, for tomorrow will bring its own worries. Today's trouble is enough for today." God has only given you enough grace for today's worries. If you take on tomorrow's, you're asking to borrow grace that He's not ready to give you yet. Why won't He go ahead and give it now? Because God knows a little secret that you do not: you're going to need it tomorrow.

Patience, friend. One day at a time. It's the secret to contentment.

Lord, I find it hard to wait. As You revive my God-given gifts and talents—things I haven't done in years—I'll be patient. I'll wait on You. I want this, Lord, but in Your time. Amen.

I Get a Kick Out of You

Train up a child in the way he should go;
even when he is old he will not depart from it.
PROVERBS 22:6 ESV

I think you'd make the perfect clown, Harvey."

"Clown?" Well, this was a suggestion he'd never heard before.

"Yes." His wife patted him on the back. "You know how I've been volunteering in the children's department at church? Well, we're doing a circus-themed Vacation Bible School. We need a clown, and I told our director I'd ask you. We all agree you'd be perfect!"

"Oh, no. Not me. No way."

"Just think about it. And pray about it too."

"You want me to pray about becoming a clown? Is this a serious request, JoAnne?"

"I've never been more serious in my life." Her expression softened. "And let's face it, you won't really have to act, Harve. You've been a clown your whole life."

"True, that."

"That's why we all think you'd be perfect. You're the funniest person we know. Naturally funny. We think your sense of humor will resonate with the kids. They'll never forget you."

"I'll pray about it," he said. "But no promises."

Maybe you read Harvey's story and laugh. The idea of putting on a costume and role-playing with kids is too far-fetched. But here's something to think about: your church may really need you. Oh, maybe not in a clown suit, but perhaps to pray for the little ones. Or to fix snacks. Or to help with crafts. Or to teach Bible lessons.

As Harvey's wife said, "Think about it. Pray about it." But don't be surprised when you find yourself pulling that clown outfit out of the mothballs!

Lord, it's a stretch to think I'd end up serving at the church after all these years, but I'm open to the possibilities. Show me who, what, when, where, why, and how, Father. Then give me the energy to serve where You want me to serve! Amen.

Trust in the Lord

Trust in the LORD with all your heart;
do not depend on your own understanding.
Seek His will in all you do, and He will show you
which path to take.

PROVERBS 3:5–6 NLT

D o you trust God?"

The question stopped Henry cold. He squirmed in his seat and tugged at his collar.

"Do you trust God?" the pastor asked once again, gripping the edges of the pulpit and staring out at the congregation. "Because if you do, you'll stop worrying about tomorrow. You'll realize that His promises are yes and amen. You will remember that God's ways are above your ways. His understanding is far superior to your own."

Henry shifted his position once again, more uncomfortable than ever. Was it getting warm in here, or was it just him? Why did the pastor have to go there, anyway? Surely everyone struggled with trusting God. After his recent cancer diagnosis, Henry had a legitimate reason to worry, to doubt. Right? It was natural. Normal.

"Do you trust Me?" The words seemed to

drift down from above—not from the pulpit, but someplace higher. "Do you trust Me, Henry?"

He swallowed hard as the answer drifted through his mind: *If I live, I live for You, Lord. If I die, I spend eternity with You.*

Peace settled over him like a warm blanket. Really, when Henry thought about it like that, fear didn't stick around long. All his days were numbered by the Lord. How could he help but put his faith in the One who loved him most?

"You can trust Him," the pastor said.

And for the first time in a while, Henry believed it.

Maybe you are in a tough season too. Perhaps you're dealing with a health crisis or a financial matter that has you in a quandary. You can trust Him, friend . . . even now.

I might not be feeling it, Lord, but I choose to place my trust in You. Who else could I turn to, after all? You are looking out for me in a way that no one else can, or will. How grateful I am! Amen.

Who Wrote the Book of Love?

For the word of God is living and active, sharper than any two-edged sword, piercing to the division of soul and of spirit, of joints and of marrow, and discerning the thoughts and intentions of the heart.

HEBREWS 4:12 ESV

"You know, Galen, that Bible is meant to be opened every now and again."

"Hmm?" Galen looked up from his TV show. "What did you say, Donn?"

His brother pointed to the dusty Bible on the coffee table. "When you take the time to open it, the dust falls off. And a few other things fall off too. Just saying."

"Ah. Right. The Bible." Galen turned back to his show, his thoughts a million miles away.

Oh, friends! The Bible is sitting there, ready to be read!

It's the map to guide you every day of your life.

It's the manual for how to get through any broken relationship.

It's the story of mankind from beginning to end.

It's a book filled with stories of wonder and awe, majesty and transformation.

And yet, it's also a book that many people ignore. They let their Bible sit idly on the bedside table or bookshelf, gathering dust.

If you knew that your Bible would give you courage to get through the day, would you read it?

If you realized it had the formula for financial peace, would you apply it?

If you understood that the Word of God offered a glimpse into heaven's greatest plan for humanity, would you delve into that story and find your place in it?

Dear friend! The Bible is more than a guide. It's filled with the very words of your Creator, the one who formed you in your mother's womb. It's action-packed, loaded with wisdom from the ages. And best of all, it's yours for the taking.

Read it.

Absorb it.

Love it.

Share it.

During this retirement season, get into the Word as never before, and then watch as it transforms every area of your life!

What a gift You've given us, Lord! I cherish Your Word. May it guide my every thought and action. Amen.

HOW TO:

Take the world's longest coffee break:

Retire!

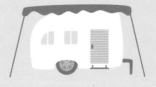

REAWAKEN

Reawaken

Therefore it says, "Awake, O sleeper, and arise
from the dead, and Christ will shine on you."
EPHESIANS 5:14 ESV

Retirement is often a season when sleeping things wake up, when dormant things spring back to life. Whether you're talking about dreams, relationships, or opportunities, God can use these years to stir you back to action, back to caring, back to hoping. So, what does it mean to reawaken? Let's take a look.

Re-: again
Awaken: shake off slumber, rise, come awake,
come alive

Maybe you've had this happen before: You wake up in the middle of the night, realize it's not morning yet, then doze back off. You sleep a few more hours, then wake at the appropriate time. The sunlight streams in from the window, casts its beams on your face, and shouts, "It's time! Get up!"

That's how it is when you allow God to fully control the seasons of your life. He knows when it's time for slumber and He knows when it's time to rouse you. At just the right moment, He will bring you from a reclining position to sitting straight up, ready to greet a new dawn. He will shine His light so brightly that it leaves little doubt in your mind about that season you're about to step into.

Wake, sleeper! It's time!

So, what is God reawakening in you during this special season? A deeper commitment to Him? A dream that has been dormant? Romance, perhaps? A reignited relationship with your spouse?

Even if your friendships are slumbering at the moment, God can zap them with spiritual caffeine. Even if your marriage is dying on the vine, the Author of heaven and earth can spring it to life once more. Even if your hope is fading, your precious heavenly Father can resurrect it. He's got the perfect moment in mind to raise you from your slumber, set your feet on the ground below, and brush the sleep from your eyes. Trust His timing. Be ready to take action. Be excited about the possibilities!

Lord, I trust You with my seasons. You know when I sleep and when I rise. You have a plan to reawaken so many things inside of me, and I choose to trust You with every single one. Amen.

Hey, Good Lookin'

Then the LORD God said, "It is not good that the man should be alone; I will make him a helper fit for him."
GENESIS 2:18 ESV

"Get remarried? But Mom, I had no idea you were dating anyone."

Darla stared into her daughter's concerned eyes as she responded, "Oh, I'm not! That's not my point."

"You're not dating anyone . . . but you want to get married?"

"I just meant someday," Darla explained. "I've been giving it a lot of thought, and I think it's time to start praying to that end. If God has someone out there for me, I want to be open to it. We've never talked about this before, so I thought I'd make an announcement that I'm open to the idea, that's all."

"Ah. Well, I think that would be awesome, Mom." The edges of her daughter's lips tipped up in a smile. "If anyone deserves a true happily-ever-after, you do. Now I know how to pray."

"Thanks, honey. This season of my life has been great so far. You know how much I love to travel and try new things. But I think it would be even better if I had someone to share the experiences with."

"Besides me, you mean?"

"Touché, kid." She patted her daughter's hand and laughed. "Touché."

Perhaps you can relate to Darla's internal ponderings. You're currently single and wishing you had someone to share your days (and your life) with. You're blessed with friends and family, but you're definitely open to romance.

God sees your desires, and He cares! There's no way to know if He will supply a mate or will grace you through this season, just you and Him, but you can trust Him, regardless. He's the lover of your soul, the one who adores you more than life itself. So, lean into Him as you pray for a mate, and watch as He gives you all you need . . . and more.

I trust You, Lord! Thanks for loving me so much. I bring You my heart. However You choose to fill it is just fine with me! Amen.

Band of Gold

An excellent wife who can find?
She is far more precious than jewels.
PROVERBS 31:10 ESV

It's hard to explain," Craig said. "But Deena and I are . . ." He smiled as he thought through his next words.

"Going on a trip?" his best friend, Lonnie, asked.

"No. Well, yes. We do love to travel, but it's something else. We're . . . we're like honeymooners all over again. The past few weeks we've really come together in a way neither of us anticipated. Things have been . . . great."

"Ah, I see." Lonnie quirked a brow. "Things are good in the romance department? Is that what you're saying?"

"Yes, it's hard to explain, but ever since that marriage retreat we went to, we've both been trying harder. We're not bickering or squabbling over every little thing these days. In fact, we . . ." He felt his cheeks grow warm. "Anyway, like I said, we're like honeymooners all over again."

Lonnie cleared his throat. "Alrighty then. What's the name of this marriage retreat? I think maybe Peg and I need to sign up, and the sooner the better!"

Maybe you have a desire to grow your marriage, to make things better. You're tired of the nitpicking, the squabbling, the distance that has grown between you. You're done with simply cohabitating in the same home. That's not enough anymore. You've set your sights on something bigger, grander.

Now that you're in your retirement years, you genuinely want things with your spouse to be better—not just externally, but down to the core. And they can be! It will take effort, but with the Lord's help, you can reawaken your marriage. You can fall in love all over again. And you can do so in a way that makes you feel fresh, young, and very much alive.

Commit your relationship to Him, then watch as He takes your offering and grows it into a thing of beauty.

Lord, I want the strongest possible marriage.
I don't want these years to be squandered on
arguing or growing apart. Instead, I long for the
best possible relationship with my spouse. Help us,
I pray. Amen.

Whole Lotta Shakin' Goin' On

I can do all things through him who strengthens me.

PHILIPPIANS 4:13 ESV

can't." Lena shrugged. "That's all there is to it. I just can't."

"How do you know?" her son asked. "You haven't even applied for the mortgage yet. How do you know they'll turn you down?"

"I just know."

"But that's just it, Mom," he argued. "You don't know because you won't ask. And if you won't ask, then you'll never know for sure. See?"

She shrugged, but in her heart she knew it was impossible. Totally, completely impossible. Why couldn't her son see that too?

Still, she had to wonder what it might be like to own her own home. Lena could almost see herself setting up house in a place of her very own, where she could paint the walls. And plant a garden. And invite the grandkids over for a baking day in a spacious kitchen. Having her own place would be lovely, but right now it just felt impossible.

But what if her son was right? She would never know unless she tried.

Perspective. It's a wonderful thing, isn't it? A shift in perspective can turn a bad day into a good one. It can encourage you to offer forgiveness to someone you claimed you'd never forgive. A change in attitude or perspective can bring hope to a hopeless situation and can reinvigorate your spirit, even when you've been feeling down in the dumps. Most importantly, a shift in perspective can give you the wherewithal to do something you felt was totally impossible. Change your thinking . . . change your outcome. (Hey, you know it's true! You'll never defeat those giants if you're convinced you can't!)

Why is perspective so important to the retiree? Because you've got amazing adventures ahead! Today, take inventory. What areas of your life could use a perspective shift?

Lord, I give You the areas of my life that have been like concrete to me. I've felt so stuck! But no more. I'll shift my thinking. I'll garner hope. I'll wait for the infusion of Your Spirit. Together, the impossible will be possible! Amen.

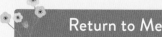

Return to Me

I rejoiced with those who said to me,
"Let us go to the house of the LORD."
PSALM 122:1 NIV

"How long has it been since you connected with people from the church?" Everett asked.

Gabe shrugged. "Years, really. Regina never really wanted to go, and I got tired of arguing with her. It was no fun to sit in the pew by myself. I tried that off and on for years but finally gave up."

"You won't be alone this time," Everett said. "You can sit with me. Then I won't be by myself either. Though, I've kind of gotten used to it since Naomi passed. I think you'll really enjoy it. Our services lately have been so . . . powerful. Anointed. There's really no other word to describe it. I always leave feeling better than when I came. And I think you'll enjoy the new pastor. He's young, but filled with passion, which is good."

That sounded good to Gabe. Really good, in fact.

Maybe you've been away from church for a season, like Gabe. Perhaps personal struggles have kept you separated from others. Maybe you've even given up on online services as well. You don't seem to get as much out of them as you once did. It's just easier to skip it.

You'll find God's thoughts in Hebrews 10:25: "Let us not neglect our church meetings, as some people do, but encourage and warn each other, especially now that the day of His coming back again is drawing near" (TLB).

Maybe it's time to go back. Get involved—not just with the people, but with the Lord. Reconnect with Him in corporate worship—through songs, the message, and prayer. Who knows? It may be exactly what you need to jumpstart something new and exciting.

Jesus, I'll confess that I don't always want to stay connected—to people or to You. Sometimes I get stuck in a rut and forget how much better my life can be if I'll spend time in Your presence. If You want me within those walls, give me the wherewithal to go back, I pray. Amen.

What a Wonderful World

*A joyful heart is good medicine, but a
crushed spirit dries up the bones.*
PROVERBS 17:22 ESV

Are you ready, friend? Ready for this wonderful, adventurous season? No matter what lies ahead—romance, travel, home renovation, inner-city missions, or taking a cup of coffee to your next-door neighbor—your retirement years can be great. They are what you make them. So, make them terrific.

One last piece of advice as you step out into the great unknown: Be a joy spreader. Toss it around like seeds in fertile soil. Many in their golden years face depression, loss, or feelings of aloneness. The transition to retirement causes fear and anxiety for some, even those who used to be bubbly and bright. They shut themselves off and don't seem open to your encouragement.

Encourage them anyway. Check in on the ones who aren't doing well. Send a quick text. Mail a card. Spread joy in every way you can.

At the supermarket.

When you take the car to the mechanic.

As you're walking the dog.

When you're going through a tough financial situation.

As you're tackling a room renovation.

Even then, with a mountain looming in front of you, you can be a joy spreader. How is this possible? The Spirit of God dwells inside you! He's infusing you—with love, peace, kindness, and all the other fruits of the Spirit. And don't forget the one that will make a lasting difference to those you come in contact with.

Joy.

It's His gift to you and to those you meet. So, as you reimagine your life, as you reinvent yourself and rediscover who you were meant to be, do it all with a smile on your face and a song in your heart. And remember the old adage: "Retire from work, but not from life" (M. K. Soni).

Lord, thank You for this season. I won't waste it!
I'll go out with joy and be led forth with peace,
spreading hope to everyone I come in contact
with. Because Your Spirit resides inside of me,
I know this is possible. Thank You, heavenly
Father! Amen.

LIVE YOUR FAITH

Dear Friend,

This book was prayerfully crafted with you, the reader, in mind. Every word, every sentence, every page was thoughtfully written, designed, and packaged to encourage you—right where you are this very moment. At DaySpring, our vision is to see every person experience the life-changing message of God's love. So, as we worked through rough drafts, design changes, edits, and details, we prayed for you to deeply experience His unfailing love, indescribable peace, and pure joy. It is our sincere hope that through these Truth-filled pages your heart will be blessed, knowing that God cares about you—your desires and disappointments, your challenges and dreams.

He knows. He cares. He loves you unconditionally.

BLESSINGS!
THE DAYSPRING BOOK TEAM

Additional copies of this book and
other DaySpring titles can be purchased
at fine retailers everywhere.
Order online at <u>dayspring.com</u>
or
by phone at 1-877-751-4347

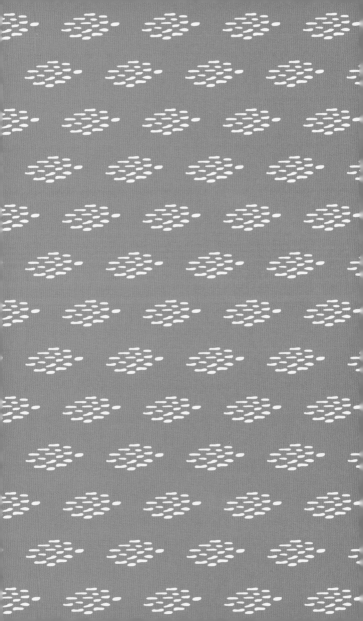

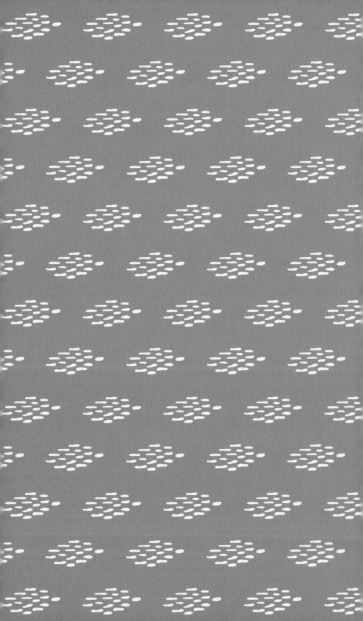